Bl ℓ 1/

D1108075

PARLIAMENTARY REFORM 1933–1960

A Survey of Suggested Reforms

PARLIAMENTARY REFORM

1933–1960

A SURVEY OF SUGGESTED REFORMS

PUBLISHED FOR
THE HANSARD SOCIETY BY
CASSELL · LONDON

CASSELL & COMPANY LTD

35 Red Lion Square . London WC1

and at

MELBOURNE · SYDNEY · TORONTO

CAPETOWN

JOHANNESBURG · AUCKLAND

———

First published 1961

Printed by J. W. Arrowsmith Ltd., Bristol

F.761

CONTENTS

CONTENTS

FOREWORD

IN 1958, the Council of the Hansard Society for Parliamentary Government decided to investigate a question which in a sense has been topical since the establishment of Parliament. In general terms it is the question whether at any given period in our history the current arrangements and methods whereby the British Parliament conducts its business and carries out its responsibilities are adequate for these purposes. The flexibility of the British Parliamentary system is one of its glories and its history is a record of continuous change.

During the past half-century, social and economic changes have been so widespread and rapid (and this has been especially true during the past thirty years), that the question outlined above has been under continuous discussion. A very large number of suggestions have been made for changes, great and small, in the Parliamentary set-up.

In order to study these proposals the reader must search in many publications, including of course the voluminous records of Hansard.

It was therefore decided that a book should be prepared whose pages would contain a representative collection of these proposals arranged under appropriate headings and linked together by objective comment.

While the period covered extended roughly over the previous twenty-five years, occasional references to major proposals for reform prior to 1933 were not excluded. But such retrospective references are rare and brief, as it was felt that maximum usefulness could be attained only if the subject was kept within manageable proportions.

As the titles to the Chapters show, the terms of reference have been discussed under certain broad subject headings. Within these headings, a limited amount of overlapping was inevitable; the question of political parties, for example, occurs on several occasions outside the main chapter devoted to the subject. The book should in consequence be read as a whole, not as a series of self-contained essays.

No attempt has been made to comment in any way upon the virtues or weaknesses of the various criticisms and proposals studied. The aim has been to provide a classified and indexed survey of the facts, which will serve as a basis for further comment and discussion. The various 'conclusions' within and at the end of each chapter are therefore nothing more than an attempt to clarify, analyse and sum up the opinions of others. Similarly, those proposals put forward from an extremely partisan point of view and which would appear to be little more than propaganda for some particular body or interest have either been ignored or mentioned only in passing.

The starting-point, and the subject to which all the work returns, is Parliament itself—in particular the House of Commons. Such factors as local government, external pressure groups and the Civil Service proper have been mentioned briefly if and when their respective influences have appeared to have a direct bearing on our subject—the reform of Parliament.

The House of Lords presented a special problem. It was decided that House of Lords reform—which comprises a subject on its own and was already the central topic discussed in a Hansard Society publication in 1954—should be omitted. However, in order to avoid the impression that our Parliament has only one chamber, an Appendix dealing with some of the proposals for reforming the Lords has been included.

In a lecture given shortly before he died, Harold Laski said that if all the criticisms of Parliament (he was speaking in particular of the House of Commons) were added up, one's resulting impression might well be that Parliament should be abolished. Yet the alternative, he continued, appeared to be the concentration camp.* This seems to have been the conviction underlying, to a greater or lesser degree, all the attacks on our parliamentary system. The vital theme of criticisms voiced and remedies suggested has been: how can the present system be strengthened and improved, so that it may long continue as the centre of British constitutional

*H. J. Laski: *Reflections on the Constitution*, M.U.P. 1951, p. 16.

democracy? The more recent proposed answers to that question —differing greatly in type and scope—are collated here.

At the time when this work was first ready for the Press a prolonged strike took place in the printing trade. But, since the House of Commons Select Committee on Procedure was about to produce its report (March 1959) pressure was put on the Council to make available to students and others the results of the research work into this subject. A special edition of 500 copies in photostat form entitled *Parliamentary Reform 1933-1958—A Survey of Suggested reforms* was therefore produced at thirty shillings, and immediately sold out.

The demand for this work underlined the wisdom of the Council's decision to investigate this subject, but it was impracticable to produce further copies of the special edition which in any case was bulky and of a non-permanent character.

It was therefore decided to invite the research team to review their labours and produce a revised edition in permanent book form. This is the book you are now reading. Many parts of the photostat edition have been substantially overhauled and much new material has been added. It is in fact virtually a new book whose ancestor is the now out-of-print photostat volume.

Even whilst proofs were being prepared for the printer, fresh suggestions for parliamentary reform were coming to light, and new books bearing on the subject (e.g. A. H. Hanson's *Parliament and Public Ownership*, Cassell, 1961) were being published. It is therefore only fair to concede at the outset that a work of this nature can never be absolutely up-to-date; and the present survey should be regarded as complete up to about the autumn of 1960.

OCTOBER 1960   STEPHEN KING-HALL

I

Elections and Representation

(a) INTRODUCTION: FRANCHISE AND CONSTITUENCIES

A British General Election is regarded nowadays as an eminently serious matter. Not only does the average elector appreciate the importance of the occasion, but the psephologists and sociologists have won possession of Eatanswill. Farce is out, facts are in: since the last war, Nuffield College has sponsored inquiries into each General Election, and there have been many other serious studies in the same or related fields. Press and sound-radio give full coverage of elections. Further, the tremendously increased importance of 'television politics' has now made its first real impact on the electorate, to such an extent, in fact, that very few homes in the country remained in complete ignorance of, or indifference to, the major issues at stake on 8th October 1959.[1]

The potential significance of those proposals for electoral reform which are still open to consideration scarcely needs emphasizing, therefore. In the nineteenth century and the earlier years of the present century the focus for reforming activity in the matter of representation was, of course, the franchise. The principal goals of reform have now been reached in that respect, and the arguments advanced about a hundred years ago—both for and against an extended franchise—make strange reading to-day.[2] Yet the chapter is not completely closed. Just prior to the 1959 General Election, a committee reporting for the Labour Party on 'The Younger Generation' brought up anew the question of reducing the qualifying age for the franchise from twenty-one to eighteen.[3] Support for the idea was expressed at a meeting of the Labour Party's National Executive Committee in January 1960, and Emrys Hughes subsequently attempted, unsuccessfully, to make eighteen the

For Notes and References see pages 23–26

minimum statutory age for parliamentary franchise.[4] People called up for military service, he argued, should be entitled to vote; moreover, 'at the age of eighteen the young people of to-day are citizens', and therefore entitled to the full benefits of citizenship. Anthony Wedgwood Benn, in support of the Bill, suggested that such an extension would help convince the young folk that Parliament was no mere ceremonial sword, but rather an instrument they might use for their own purpose. Alan Thompson hoped that the Bill, on becoming an Act, would mark a further landmark in the progress towards *full* democracy. In the event, the Bill was not passed; despite a by no means negligible amount of support for the idea, it cannot be said that accusations of a 'partial franchise' form the major part of current proposals for electoral reform.[5] A strong body of opinion, even amongst young people, supports the thesis that twenty-one is a fair minimum age-qualification, and that the principle of 'one man, one vote' rests safely on that basis.

It has been suggested that, with regard to the franchise, the one really contentious issue likely to arise concerns university representation.[6] Winston Churchill said in 1952 that it remained the declared intention of the Government to legislate on the subject, and already in their election programmes of 1950 and 1951 the Conservatives had promised the restoration of the university franchise.[7] The question slumbers somewhat for the time being, although A. P. Herbert briefly revived the matter in his 1958 election address to East Harrow. If it is raised again, D. E. Butler's prophecy of 'contention' will undoubtedly be realized. As he points out, 'the closeness of the results of the elections of 1950 and 1951 will certainly add to the vehemence of Labour opposition to any move to re-establish the university seats'.

The question of constituency boundaries would appear to have been largely settled—temporarily, at least—by the acceptance of permanent bodies known as Boundary Commissioners, who undertake periodic, impartial reviews of boundaries.[8] Nevertheless, there had been some explosive comment and discussion prior to the 1958 Act—not only from Members who feared (sometimes correctly) that redistribution would mean the loss of their seats, but from local authorities who felt that the Commissioners' changes had not taken local opinion sufficiently into consideration. Under the 1958 Act, if 100 electors or an interested organization object to a proposed change, an inquiry must be held, unless there was an inquiry prior to the actual announcement of the proposal. But, as P. G. Richards has said, there is still no means of appeal against the suggestion of the Commissioners except to the Home Secretary or to Parliament—where the Government has in any case the power of its parliamentary majority to enforce its wishes. Richards continues: 'Should the decisions of the Commissions be open to review and, if so, by what kind of body?' Then again, if redistribution is completed shortly before a General Election (as in 1955), is this fair to Members and their local supporters who have to face, unprepared, a changed electorate? To minimize such inconvenience, the suggestion has been put forward that redistribution should not be too frequent (the 1958 Act went some way towards meeting this demand) and that the Commissioners should begin their work immediately after a General Election. There is fairly widespread agreement that all constituencies cannot consist of exactly equal electorates (numerically speaking), if natural and local authority boundaries are not to be completely ignored; and also that Scotland, Wales and rural areas must have a smaller quota of electors than the rest of the country.[9] This acquiescence in the numerical inequalities of electorates is challenged only by those who, associating the latter with the existence of single-member constituencies, use those same inequalities as another argument in favour of electoral reform. Thus, J. F. S. Ross writes that 'the single-member constituency is a rigid unit that is quite conspicuously unsuited to the immense variety of conditions, urban and rural, to be found in any modern country, and . . . is, in practice, incompatible with the principles of equal electorates. Where all constituencies are confined to the return of a solitary Member each, you *cannot* secure equal electorates . . . unless you are prepared to draw constituency boundaries with a ruthless disregard alike for common sense and local feeling'.[10] Ross goes on to argue the merits of a five-member constituency under proportional representation.

A subject which could be raised again is that of colonial Members. A scheme for Malta was agreed upon which would involve the presence of Maltese representatives at Westminster, and on 7th December 1949, Harold Davies suggested to the Commons that all colonies should send Members direct to Westminster. The suggestion was rejected, partly for the strong reason that the colonies were in any case more interested in self-government.[11]

(b) THE PROGRESS OF ELECTORAL REFORM

The progress in the present century of electoral reform has been described, *inter alia*, by Ross, by the late R. W. G. Mackay and by D. E. Butler.[12] Most of the recommendations of the three Speaker's Conferences on electoral reform (in 1916–17, 1929–30 and 1944 respectively) have now passed into law. But certain of the issues raised are still outstanding. A skeleton summary of the course of events regarding these live issues—notably proportional representation (P.R.) and the alternative vote (A.V.)—follows.

The first Speaker's Conference proposed, among other things, the adoption of proportional representation by the single transferable vote (that is, preferential voting and quota counting) for elections in all boroughs returning three or more Members each, including London outside the City, and the adoption of the alternative vote for elections in single-member constituencies contested by two or more candidates.[13] These 'bold and even startling innovations' (in Ross's words) were recommended by the Conference; but when in 1917–18 the Government put through the Representation of the People Bill that embodied the recommendations of the Conference, the clauses concerning proportional representation and the alternative vote were left to free votes of the House. After lengthy parliamentary battles involving both Houses, the clauses were defeated, P.R. remaining only for the two- and three-membered University constituencies.

The first Speaker's Conference produced an impressive series of unanimous recommendations; the second was largely sterile. It was set up in 1929 by Ramsay MacDonald when he held office with Liberal support. The General Election of May 1929 had proved disastrous for the Liberals and it was not surprising that they pressed MacDonald for a measure of electoral reform as the price of their support. However, in the second Speaker's Conference, the participants were apparently entirely lacking in 'the admirable temper and conciliatory disposition' which the Speaker had found in 1917;[14] no agreement was reached on the issues (which included P.R. and the A.V.) before the Conference. In spite of the

4

lack of agreement the Government announced, in the King's Speech on 28th October 1930 'a measure of Electoral Reform'. This appears to have been promised to the Liberals in return for their support in the House of Commons.[15] On 17th January 1931, the text of a bill was published, the main feature of which was the introduction of the alternative vote. Labour support for the latter system was only half-hearted: *The Times* commented, on 4th February 1931, that the Second Reading debate made it clear that 'no party except the Liberal party really wants any change in the electoral system at all'. In a debate on electoral reform held on 6th December 1933, Mr. Attlee said that although he had voted for the alternative vote in the debates on the bill, he had disapproved of it and only voted for it because of the 'bargain' with the Liberals.[16] However, in spite of some adverse votes and abstentions by Labour Members, the bill passed the House of Commons, only to be rejected by the Lords. The Government intended to push through the bill under the provisions of the Parliament Act, but in August the Government fell and the bill proceeded no further.

For a long time thereafter the electoral system excited little interest in Parliament. However, during the last war, it was apparent that there would be urgent problems arising at the end of hostilities, particularly concerning the need for redistribution of seats. A third Speaker's Conference was therefore set up in 1944. It passed a great many agreed resolutions which have consequently been enacted, but resolutions concerning proportional representation and the alternative vote were decisively defeated: a resolution to introduce P.R. generally by twenty-five votes to four, a resolution to introduce P.R. experimentally by twenty-four votes to five, and a resolution in favour of the A.V. by twenty votes to five. The minority consisted of the Liberal and Independent members, whilst some Labour Members abstained on the vote concerning the A.V.

In spite of their defeat in 1945 the Conservatives' faith in the electoral system was in no way shaken—they were willing, as Butler has said, 'to await the day when they once again would benefit by its natural exaggerations'.[17] The Representation of the People Act, 1948, excited great party bitterness because it went beyond the recommendations of the Speaker's Conference by abolishing University seats and the business vote, but its results now appear to be accepted, temporarily at least.

The most recent proceedings regarding electoral reform—Sir Winston Churchill's speech of 1950 and the canvassing of the alternative vote system—will be discussed below in the section on *The Prospects for Electoral Reform.*

(c) PROPORTIONAL REPRESENTATION

The fundamental question in electoral reform to-day is that of the voting system used, and although the story of the 'progress' of reform in this century shows a steady movement away from proportional representation and the alternative vote (unanimously recommended by the first Speaker's Conference), the latter systems still have their devoted, active advocates.

The general position taken up by protagonists of reform is stated by Ross as follows:

> Systems of voting and of counting votes are the mechanism by means of which the country records and measures its re-actions to the political issues of the day. As with all recording and measuring devices, therefore, it is important that these systems should be as accurate, as reliable, and as impartial as we can make them. To tamper with them—or to tolerate the continuance of their known defects—in the interests of a particular party or policy should be regarded as one of the things that are simply not done: it is on a par with using false weights and measures.[18]

The premise on which all argument for electoral reform rests is that Members should be returned more exactly in proportion to the votes cast than under the present system in this country.[19] It has been frequently demonstrated that the present system is unfair in that Members may be elected on minority votes, and that the number of seats obtained in the House is seldom in exact proportion to the percentage of votes received in the country.[20] Gilbert Murray once said that it was a condition of our keeping the Parliamentary system that the voting system should be fair—not ideally fair, but decently fair. Only proportional representation could meet

6

this need; the alternative vote would not be adequate: 'We want a system which will give an assurance to the average citizen that he will have a chance of voting for a representative of whom he really approves, and that, if outvoted, he will be outvoted by a real majority.'[21] As might be expected, the Liberal party, the worst sufferers from the inequalities of the present system, also uses the argument of 'fairness'. The Liberals are not tied to definite proposals, but have suggested proportional representation by the single transferable vote, with the alternative vote in rural areas, as 'the fairest way out'.[22] At Speaker's Conferences the Liberals have, of course, consistently supported P.R. or, as a second-best the A.V. Ross argues that proportional representation, as well as being less clumsy and capricious in its action than the present 'first-past-the-post' system, would give more scope for the elector to exercise actively his choice and shrewdness, and would result in a better-balanced, more gifted House of Commons.[23] The use of P.R. would avoid foregone conclusions, would afford the elector a choice of persons as well as of parties (because in multi-member constituencies each party would run more than one candidate), would abolish caucus-controlled safe seats, and would tend to eliminate inferior candidates.[24]

Lakeman and Lambert add that the Member would himself be given a greater degree of independence. They also deal at length with the familiar criticisms of the technical aspects of P.R., since some of those who support the reform in theory are doubtful as to whether it would work in practice. Lakeman and Lambert argue that it is not too difficult for the voters to understand, that it does not take too long to carry out the count, that it is not excessively costly, and that it is possible to overcome the difficulties of by-elections when one Member retires or dies in a multi-member constituency. Far from encouraging abstentions on account of its supposed difficulties (the authors claim), P.R. would in practice lead to fewer abstainers: voters would not feel that the result was a foregone conclusion, and would be pleased at the wider choice of candidates offered them on the ballot paper.[25]

L. S. Amery, following the recommendations of the first Speaker's Conference, favoured the use of P.R. in the larger cities.[26] Churchill also, in 1935, spoke in favour of P.R. in the larger cities. R. Muir advocated the system with the single transferable vote in constituencies returning from three to seven members.[27] Another argument sometimes used in favour of P.R. is that when, as in 1945 or 1931, one party receives far more than its share of seats, the opposition is seriously weakened and is liable to be ineffective.[28] Most supporters of P.R. point out that a system which leads to such inequitable results as that of 1945 undermines the prestige of Parliament. A Parliament in which the Government, though it has a large majority in the House of Commons, has the support of only a minority of the electorate cannot properly claim to have the nation's confidence or accurately reflect its views.

(d) CRITICISMS OF PROPORTIONAL REPRESENTATION

Critics of P.R. attack the very basis of the arguments of its supporters. Ross recognizes this: 'The crucial divergence is between those who think it vital that representation shall be a living reality, and those who think it of little importance so long as we get what they call "strong government". This is a clash of opinion that threatens the stability of the whole electoral system.'[29] Some examples of these criticisms of the whole aim of P.R. follow. *The Economist*, commenting on the report of the 1944 Speaker's Conference, said that the rejection of P.R. was right: the chief strength of the British system of government was that Cabinets could usually rely on the assured support of a majority in the House of Commons. The purpose of elections was not to secure an exactly representative House, but to put into power the Government the electors like most or dislike least.[30]

J. P. Mayer, in a review of Ross's *Parliamentary Representation*, doubted whether P.R. would work in a modern mass state.[31] The author, Mayer contends, is clearly antagonistic towards parties: but without firmly organized political parties it is difficult to see how the modern mass electorate can be transformed into manageable units. It is more profitable to think of ways in which an adequate representation of the electorate might be achieved *within* the party machines. Mayer also discounts the arguments that the present system, with its exaggerations of majorities, leads to a weak opposition: he points out that, in fact, an 'exaggerated' or 'false' majority cannot disregard a strong minority, nor a majority of votes against the Government in the country. Arithmetically

8

the voters are disenfranchised, but actually they do count. There is also, according to Mayer, no doubt that the two-party system is 'the unwritten law underlying the new parliamentary order of things in England' (G. M. Trevelyan in his Romanes lecture of 1926), and if proportional representation upset this system it could also upset the Constitution. The view of supporters of P.R. and of many other writers on the electoral system, that the main object of the House of Commons is 'to reflect the views expressed by the electorate' (a dictum of the second Speaker's Conference), is also not universally accepted. It is argued that this view ignores the rôle of the House of Commons as an organ for the *formulation* of the social will. Whereas proportional representation sets out to mirror, or 'photograph', the undecided mind of the electorate, what general elections should result in are definite and decisive majorities.[32] Similarly Harold Nicolson, while admitting that the present voting system and the two-party system are logically indefensible, claims that they are the best means of running representative institutions.[33] Harold Laski, as a 'strong believer in a stable executive',[34] also criticized proportional representation, and he did not admit that Parliament should mirror national opinion. He believed that P.R., with its probable multiplication of parties, would lead to excessive compromise. This argument is developed by other writers, for instance Michael Stewart, who writes: 'Under proportional representation the elector would know that, whatever party he voted for, there would be little likelihood of its policy being carried out; for the Government would be a coalition whose nature and working would be unpredictable.'[35] Ivor Bulmer-Thomas also argues that P.R. would make for weak Government and tend to substitute 'backstairs intrigue' for open debate; it would, moreover, weaken the link between the Member and his constituency.[36] The same writer concedes, however, that P.R. might be tried experimentally. M. R. Curtis also argues against the system, on the grounds that the government would be produced by party bargaining over which the elector had no control.[37] Finally, not a few impartial observers of the campaigns for and against the system of proportional representation hesitate to accept the evidence of its success in other countries as conclusive proof that it would function well here. What is good for Tasmania is not necessarily good for the United Kingdom—and vice versa.

Lakeman and Lambert endeavour to counter criticisms of proportional representation in Chapter VIII of their *Voting in Democracies*. They argue that the system does not itself create a multiplicity of parties, but rather secures fair representation for the parties that exist for other reasons. Tasmania still has only. two parties and some Independents after half a century of P.R. On the other hand, the French voters tend to divide among the parties, and the use of a majority system has never checked this tendency. Lakeman and Lambert favour the spirit of compromise that P.R. might tend to produce, as in Scandinavian countries; they are prepared for coalition: 'a coalition backed by a majority of voters is preferable to a single-party government supported only by a minority'.[38] In answer to the critics who point to the ineffective minority Governments of 1924 and 1929, they refer to three periods when government without an assured Parliamentary majority worked well: 1846–52, 1886–92, and 1910–15.[39]

(e) THE ALTERNATIVE VOTE[40]

The adoption of proportional representation would be a thorough-going reform of the electoral system involving a complete re-drawing of constituency boundaries, and it would probably have far-reaching effects on our political life. The alternative vote system, on the other hand, could be applied within the existing electoral framework, and its effects would probably be less drastic than those of P.R. The alternative vote would improve the prospects of 'fair' electoral results without offering the more exact relationship between seats and votes obtained by proportional representation. The former system has been put forward as a compromise solution (in the Labour Government's Bill of 1931); was recommended in certain areas by the first Speaker's Conference; and has been canvassed from time to time up to the present day. Its distinction is that it has been suggested not only by the Liberals or by writers on political matters (as Ross, for example, advocates P.R.), but also, at various times, by some members of both major parties.

An article in *The Economist* of 10th June 1944, though approving of the third Speaker's Conference's rejection of P.R., said that if three-cornered contests resulting in the election of M.P.s by a

10

minority vote became common, the case for the A.V. would be a strong one. The *Manchester Guardian* (now the *Guardian*) recommended the adoption of the alternative vote, and referred to the bill introduced by Ramsay MacDonald's Government in 1931.[41] *The Economist* returned to the subject in 1952, and again in 1958, arguing its thesis thus: 'The case for the alternative vote is that it would make policies more important in politics without disrupting the two-party system, as full proportional representation admittedly might do. It would provide the elector in the middle with an opportunity . . . to show that . . . he is not voting for extreme party measures.[42]

The question of the A.V. was raised again (in 1958) as the result of improved Liberal votes at by-elections. After the 1958 Torrington by-election, in which the Liberals won the seat from the Conservatives, Christopher Hollis contributed an article to the *Manchester Guardian* entitled 'Now the alternative vote'.[43] He argued that the Torrington result made an unanswerable case for electoral reform. Whereas it had seemed that the electorate *wanted* the two-party system, it now appeared that it wanted the end of the two-party system. Without electoral reform it was possible that the Liberals would win one fifth or even one quarter of the votes, yet still receive no more seats than today. Such an unfair result would have a deplorable effect on the prestige which Parliament holds. Hollis also pointed out that the alternative vote provided the remedy for the excessive power of the caucus within a political party. In the situation which developed at Bournemouth East, when Nigel Nicolson declined his local executive's invitation to resign, both Nicolson and the local party executive candidate could have stood as Conservative candidates under the alternative vote system. Conservative electors could then express their preference between them without the risk of letting the seat go to Labour.[44] Hollis similarly referred to disagreements within the Labour Party: the proposed new system would enable the electors to decide between rival Labour candidates (and policies) instead of leaving the matter in the hands of the party caucus.[45] The subject was also ventilated about the same time in correspondence to *The Times*. G. Beyfus pointed out that recent by-elections showed many electors wished to vote for a third party. The alternative vote would enable them to vote for the candidate of their choice without

11

fear that by so doing they would merely help a candidate they opposed.[46] In a leading article which concluded ensuing correspondence, *The Times* refused to be committed beyond the opinion that 'it is fair to probe for defects in a system of election (i.e., the present one) which produces admittedly distorted ratios between seats and votes'.[47]

(f) CRITICISMS OF THE ALTERNATIVE VOTE

In the first place, the system is criticized as inadequate by supporters of proportional representation. Lakeman and Lambert voice a number of objections.[48] It means that the major parties must angle for the second preferences of those groups that have least support in the electorate. (For this reason Winston Churchill, during a debate on 2nd June 1931, described the A.V. as 'the worst of all possible plans .... The decision is to be determined by the most worthless votes given for the most worthless candidates'.)[49] Nor, it is said, is the system of the alternative vote much better than the present 'first-past-the-post' system as regards faithful reflection of the nation's wishes, or as regards the absence of uncertainty in the result. Further, it does not provide any cure for the failure of personal merit to carry weight in elections, except in such hypothetical cases as might arise if two opposed candidates of the same party contested the same seat (as might have happened at Bournemouth East in 1959). Lakeman and Lambert agree that the great merit of the alternative vote is that, although it may do nothing to improve the relation between the votes cast and the result, it could improve the relation between the votes cast and real wishes of those casting them. In other words, it does away with the 'wasted vote' bogey. Before the 1950 election the Gallup Poll asked: 'Would you vote Liberal if you thought the Liberals could win?' To this question 38 per cent replied 'Yes'—28 per cent more than those who then intended to vote Liberal, and 29 per cent more than those who actually did so at the election. That is to say, the votes of more than one quarter of the electorate were determined less by what they themselves wanted than by what they guessed most of the other electors would want.

12

(g) THE PROSPECTS FOR ELECTORAL REFORM

The introduction of proportional representation would be as great a leap in the dark as any nineteenth-century measure of reform, while the adoption of the alternative vote would lead to results which are also impossible to calculate. Lakeman and Lambert have shown how varied could be the consequences of the latter proposed reform. They point out that in 1950 most Liberal candidates were third on the poll: in this position they would be immediately eliminated under the A.V. system and therefore would not profit by it. The A.V. gives no chance to the candidate who is everyone's second choice. On the other hand, if all Conservatives gave their second choice to a Liberal, and all Labour supporters did the same, and provided the Liberals had sufficient first preferences to be in the second position on the poll, then they would be able to win every seat in the country if they acquired only just one-third of the electorate's first preferences![50] D. E. Butler has published a table showing the probable result of each general election from 1922 to 1951 if it had been held under a system of proportional representation.[51] The table reveals that only two elections in the series would have been likely to return a party with a clear working majority (namely, those of 1931 and 1935). Thus the fears of the critics of P.R.—that strong majority government would disappear—would have been realized. It is admitted, on the other hand, that the unbalanced Houses of Commons with overwhelming majorities, which were characteristic of the period, would have been averted. The necessity of coalition could, moreover, have made the House of Commons a more genuinely deliberative body. The same writer's calculations regarding the probable effects of the alternative vote bring out that the method would in no case have changed a decisive result into an indecisive one—the majority might have been reduced but would have remained adequate.[52] The majority of 1945 might have been still further exaggerated.[53] Where the results of the election were close, however, the alternative vote might have changed the situation: the narrow Labour majority of 1950 would probably have been transformed into a minority. The system would not prevent a party which won less than 50 per cent of the votes from obtaining a parliamentary majority, and it would be as likely to multiply

13

as to reduce protests at the 'injustice' of the electoral system. D. E. Butler thinks that, in all General Elections since 1923, the Liberals would have had a 'more proportionate' representation under the alternative vote. Max Beloff has suggested that electoral reform of this type would help a third party indirectly as well as directly. With 'wasted' votes wasted no longer, it is likely that people who had abandoned the third party, or never joined it, because support for it would have been ineffective or because they felt obliged to choose the 'lesser evil', would be drawn to it.[54] At the same time, 'both major parties might find that, given electoral reform, and an alternative home for some of their dissidents, unsuspected fissiparous tendencies would develop'. Beloff postulates that this possibility, as much as any calculation of seats to be lost and won immediately, makes electoral reform distasteful to both the main party machines.

However incalculable the results of electoral reform may be, there is general agreement that both major parties would suffer; in their own eyes if not in the opinion of their critics. For this reason, the prospects for reform are slight. The possibility was last raised at a high level by Winston Churchill in the Debate on the Address on 7th March 1950.[55] He said, after a General Election which had produced near stalemate, that 'we must not be blind to the anomaly which has brought to this House of Commons 186 representatives who are returned only by a minority of those who voted in their constituencies. Nor can we ... overlook the constitutional injustice done to 2,600,000 voters who ... have been able to return only nine Members. ... I therefore ... [propose] that we should set up a Select Committee to inquire into the whole question of electoral reform. ... I am well aware that it has several times been examined before, but we have never examined it in the light of a practical situation of major importance such as has now been brought about.' However, the proposal was not taken up by other Conservatives, nor was it pressed by Churchill, and it was rejected by the Government. In 1953 there were Liberal–Conservative talks on electoral reform, but these produced no concrete results.

On 1st May 1954, a letter was published in *The Times* appealing to the Government to appoint a Royal Commission on Voting. This would collect the facts regarding various voting methods so

14

that advantage could be taken 'of this vast body of experience to reconsider our own practices' and also to help and guide countries such as Malaya or Nigeria—countries having newly acquired or else approaching self-government. The letter was signed by Anthony Greenwood, W. J. Brown, D. L. Savory, Dingle Foot and other 'Sponsors of the Committee for a Royal Commission on Voting'. However, on 27th July of that same year, the Prime Minister (Sir Winston Churchill) rejected a request to set up such a Royal Commission.[56] The 'practical situation' to which Churchill referred in 1950 has disappeared; the subject as a whole has receded into the background again, although exponents of reform are by no means completely disheartened.

It seems most unlikely that one major party will attempt to impose electoral reform without the agreement of the other (though *The Economist* recommended this step in its article of 8th March 1958), or without seeking a specific mandate. Meanwhile both large parties know that they benefit from the inequalities of the present system and will hesitate to upset it. Both have kept silent in recent discussions of the alternative vote. They are concerned less with logic and fairness than with the struggle for power. The situation might change if the Liberals recovered sufficient force to make their voice heard: but will the present 'first-past-the-post' method allow a substantial Liberal recovery? The last word rests with the opponents of electoral reform.

(h) FUNCTIONAL REPRESENTATION

Representation according to people's occupations has been suggested from time to time: either as the sole form of representation, or as the method to be used for a subsidiary legislature under a scheme of devolution. Functional representation is part of the scheme of the Fascist Corporative State. It is still advocated by Sir Oswald Mosley; the latter suggests that if Parliament were elected on an occupational franchise it would be a practical rather than a political assembly, and would become more 'serious'. Hollis's third Chamber, the House of Industry, would be elected by people engaged in industry voting in 'occupational constituencies'.[57] The idea has also been supported by Amery as the system of election for his House of Industry or sub-Parliament.[58] Stewart, on the other hand, argues that functional representation might well aggravate the sectional spirit and would encourage selfishness; representatives would be expected by their constituents to press the interests of their particular 'industries' regardless of the national interest. The Fascists counter this sort of objection by saying that the Government would see that each group in the Assembly remembered the over-riding interests of the State. But if the Government controls the Assembly, then the Assembly cannot control the Government: and this was the case in Fascist Italy.[59]

(i) THE REFERENDUM AND MANDATE

Occasionally, the use of referenda in this country is suggested as a means of obtaining the expression of public opinion on specific issues. But, as C. S. Emden puts it, recent experience indicates that this method is generally regarded not only as impracticable, but also as un-English.[60]

After years of trial and debate, the doctrine of the people's mandate is still not clearly formulated. Emden thinks that it could be organized by inter-party agreement, however, in such a way that the people would be able to comment effectively on the broad outlines of projected policy at election time. Otherwise, democracy may receive a serious set-back, for the public must feel they are playing a real part in parliamentary government.[61] This line of argument, of course, assumes that 'the people' *ought* to contribute positively in such matters; many reputable supporters of democracy regard effective participation of this kind as impossible.

(j) MORE MEMBERS?

Ross has suggested that the number of Members should be increased to 'say 700'. Apart from enabling Scotland and Wales to keep their present representation, whilst removing their present unfair weighting, the increase would have other advantages: it would ease the task of redistribution of seats; it would restore the proportion of private Members in the House to a healthier figure; it would spread the burden of committee work; and it would decrease the burden of a Member's work in relation to his constituents.[62] *The Economist* has agreed that there are arguments for a larger number of Members—it would encourage closer contact between the Member and his constituents, and, as suggested by Ross, it would be the only way to restore the balance between private Members and office-holders, so distorted by the multiplication of Under-Secretaries, Parliamentary Secretaries, and Parliamentary Private Secretaries. *The Economist* suggested an electoral quota of about 50,000.[63]

On the other hand, supporters of some form of devolution argue that the Parliament at Westminster needs to be *reduced* in size. Hollis has said that Parliament is far too large as it is, and its number should be drastically reduced.[64] In *Has Parliament a Future?* the latter suggests that the maximum number of M.P.s should not much exceed a hundred.

Adams also expected that, after devolution, Parliament would be smaller.[65] The general consensus of opinion at present is against any numerical increase on the scale advocated by Ross.

(k) THE PERSONNEL OF PARLIAMENT

The question of the personnel of Parliament—the qualities of Members and of candidates—is a difficult (not to say invidious) topic on which to put forward concrete, specific suggestions for reform. It is, rather, the subject for generalization. It seems that, like *Punch*, Parliament is never as good as it used to be, and from time to time a lament goes up for the giants of yesteryear. The real or supposed shortcomings of Members are ascribed to a number of causes: the one relevant point, is the criticism of the way in which parliamentary candidates are chosen and elected.

Advocates of proportional representation believe, of course, that their multi-member constituencies would improve the quality of Members by enabling electors to express preferences between different candidates *of the same party*, whereas in single-member constituencies a Conservative voter, say, generally votes for the Conservative candidate—however much he disapproves of him personally—for fear of letting the seat go to a rival party.

Roger Fulford has noted that the powers of constituency associations have increased enormously, and that in safe seats the constituency association virtually chooses the Member: the election is a foregone conclusion.[66] This point is developed by

Nigel Nicolson in his *People and Parliament* (1958): a book which arose from the author's experience of being 'disowned' by his constituency association. Those who 'elect' the Member for, say, Bournemouth or Barnsley, are not the electors but the members of the 'caucus' of the local Conservative or Labour association. These nominate their official candidate; the latter is then automatically elected to Parliament. On the subject of a local association's right to choose its own candidate, Nicolson suggests that there is no need for revolutionary reform. The Party Headquarters should perhaps encourage selection on 'a wider basis' and over 'a longer period'. No one should be able to win the official candidature by an adroit twenty-minute interview (the method, apparently, by which he was himself chosen at Bournemouth). He also suggests a sort of 'primary' election, where two prospective candidates might 'run in harness for a year' and so work for their official candidacy.[67] Bulmer-Thomas has similarly commented on the 'tyranny' of the local party organization.[68] A group of Conservative Members and others, reporting in 1946, felt that Headquarters should not recognize a local association unless its subscribing membership represented a reasonable proportion of the Conservative electors.[69]

At heart, it must be confessed, these are largely internal matters for the party machines. It would be difficult to frame legislation to prevent what happened following the Suez operations (to Stanley Evans at Wednesbury, Sir Frank Medlicott in Norfolk, Anthony Nutting at Melton or Nigel Nicolson at Bournemouth) from occurring again—however much there is general agreement that a Member is a representative and not a delegate, and that a local association is acting tyrannically if it withdraws support from a Member who does not always see eye to eye with it.

Ross has made various suggestions about the procedures of candidacy and elections which could be implemented by legislation, though some of them might seem to be beyond the realm of practical politics. He begins by attacking the deposit of £150 required of every candidate. It presents a real barrier to poor candidates without any organizational backing; moreover, a financial barrier is not effective in preventing 'frivolous' candidatures. Not all 'freaks' are poor—nor are all rich men models of wisdom. Ross suggests, pending the abolition of the deposit, that it should be reduced to £50 and that it should be forfeited only if the candidate gains less than one-tenth of the votes, instead of the present fraction of one-eighth.[70]

In his address to the electors of East Harrow (8th December 1958), A. P. Herbert wanted to see the deposit abolished. Calling it an undemocratic device, he said that the deposit system often frightened away genuine Independents, rather than freaks. A candidate who has sought—albeit unsuccessfully—to serve his country should not be obliged to lose his £150 if he does not get enough votes. It was like an umpire saying to an unhappy batsman: 'You are out, sir. May I add that you are out for a duck? And now you will be hit on the head with a bat.'

Ross further claims that the deposit system could be abolished safely if the system of nomination were tightened up. It is at present very easy to become a candidate—apart from the deposit, one only need present a nomination paper subscribed by the signatures of ten electors with their electoral numbers. In place of this extremely cursory procedure, what is needed is a nomination system carefully designed, not merely to discourage the frivolous, but to eliminate as far as may be possible candidates personally unsuitable for membership. A deposit can never do this: integrity and ability cannot be measured by any financial device. Electors might be given more say in the choice of a candidate by a requirement that the nomination should be supported by the signatures of 500 or 1,000 electors. Such a form of nomination would serve many useful purposes. The old bogy of the 'freak' or 'frivolous' candidate would be dealt with. The genuine candidate would have no difficulty in securing the signatures, and these would show that he had real local backing. The necessity of obtaining the larger number of signatures would make the inner ring of the party more sensitive to the desirability of choosing not only a 'sound party man' but someone who is acceptable to the general run of electors.[71]

Ross also maintains that a candidate ought to be obliged to give the electors reasonably full and authentic information about himself. The returning officer should issue, on the basis of information required to be supplied by the candidate, a concise and standardized statement setting forth the essential facts about each candidate.[72] In his earlier book, *Parliamentary Representation*, Ross went further and suggested that candidates should submit voluntarily to a series of 'psychological, intelligence and aptitude tests' such as those developed by the National Institute of Industrial Psychology. The results could be published for the benefit of electors.[73] He also endorsed Laski's proposal (made in *A Grammar of Politics*) that candidates should be required to have three years' service on some local body.

However extreme some of these suggestions may seem, Ross puts them forward with the aim in mind of 'the urgent necessity' of a much higher standard of members. The danger is, of course, that any attempt to improve standards might exclude a person of real ability who has followed unorthodox paths. Would the young Winston Churchill—or the young Aneurin Bevan or Ernest Bevin —have passed Ross's tests of suitability for membership of the House of Commons?

(*l*) ELECTION EXPENSES

Criticisms of the deposit system have already been discussed. In their *Proposals for Constitutional Reform*, the group of Conservatives mentioned above went some way towards summarizing other aims of reformers in the field of election expenses. The Group (which included Viscountess Davidson, [Sir] Kenneth Pickthorn and Viscount Ridley) suggested that candidates should be forbidden by law from subscribing to the funds of their local political associations; further, that the State should refund election expenses on an approved scale, related to the area of the constituency and the size of the electorate; and that it should be illegal to exceed this amount.[74]

Ross, in Chapter 17 of his *Elections and Electors*, provides documentation for a similar argument. He points out that the average election costs of successful candidates were £763 in 1950 and £752 in 1951. The mean value of these two figures is £758. The average duration of the eight Parliaments between 1918 and 1951 (excluding that of 1935–45) was two years, ten and three-quarter months. Thus, if one assumes an expenditure of £758 every two years, ten and three-quarter months, the average election costs of Members amount to a continuous charge, year in year out, of five pounds a week. Further, these large sums may have to be found at short notice, and they are only *election* costs, not covering normal constituency outgoings or the routine expenses of parliamentary life. In these circumstances, it is inevitable that the scales are still biassed in favour of the candidate who can shoulder a large part of the burden of election expenses himself, or can find a trade union or other body to do so. Thus, it is argued that entry to the House of Commons is still governed to a considerable extent by finance rather than merit. The potential candidate who has financial backing stands a better chance than a rival who lacks that advantage. Further, a man who has to depend on the backing of a trade union or a comparable body is to that extent hampered in his freedom of action and independence of judgement. He must consider the interests and prejudices of those who meet his election bill. Legal control of maximum election expenses can do no more than prevent corrupt or over-lavish expenditure by exceptionally well-off candidates. It cannot alter the fact that a modern election contest is necessarily an expensive affair.[75]

To meet this situation Ross puts forward a scheme first suggested by him in his earlier book, *Parliamentary Representation*. He argues that the community should recognize that *bona fide* candidates perform a public service by offering themselves for election, and they should be helped to meet the high cost of so doing. What he suggests is that the State should contribute towards each candidate's costs a sum calculated on the basis of the number of valid votes recorded for that candidate. This scheme would ensure that the expenses of 'freak' candidates would not be paid. Ross records that he put forward this plan in a memorandum to the 1944 Speaker's Conference, but that the Conference stated in its Report, without giving any reasons, that it had 'agreed not to accept a proposal that the State should afford direct financial assistance to candidates'. The writer admits that the exact form of a State grant and what proportion of the total cost it should cover would need careful study. It might be enacted that the grant should not exceed, say, two-thirds of the expenses incurred.[76]

(m) ELECTION LAW MISCELLANEA

Some miscellaneous proposals for reform arising out of the state of the existing electoral law are mentioned briefly below.

(i) *Getting to the Poll*: Under Section 88 of the 1949 Representation of the People Act, it was forbidden to offer organized conveyance to the place of voting except in a limited number of registered party cars. The Conservative Government repealed Section 88 in 1958. There was considerable Labour opposition to this piece of legislation during an animated discussion in the House of Commons on 5th November of that year. One speaker said that the Government, if they felt compelled to amend existing law in this way, should not have dealt with one section in isolation. They should have combined their proposed amendment with 'other things to help to get the voters more easily to the polls'—for example, the provision of more polling stations, including mobile polling stations in country districts, and the strengthening of Section 63 of the main Act dealing with election expenses.[77] A leading article in *The Times* of 30th October 1958, had suggested that the principal effect of the repeal of Section 88 would not lie in the availability or otherwise of cars to take electors to the polls, for it could not be doubted that, in general, there would be plenty of cars for voters of all main parties. But, the article continued, much greater significance would be henceforth attached to the efficiency of party organization in constituencies: the freely permitted use of cars would entail careful planning to ensure that all potential voters for a particular party were conveyed to the polling booths. This increased influence of party organization would not be regarded by all as an unmixed blessing. D. E. Butler and R. Rose subsequently mentioned that extra Conservative votes may have been gained in Reading in October 1959 by the device of sending cars equipped with loudspeakers to greet every returning train of commuters.[78]

(ii) *Postal Voting*: Just over 2 per cent of votes cast in October 1959 were registered by post, and Butler and Rose noted some 'chronic grievances', about the state of existing legislation, which ensued.[79] Persons on holiday could not avail themselves of the postal vote—was it fair that they should have to choose between their holiday and their right to vote? The privilege of postal voting was extended only to those who had moved from one election registration district to another. Butler and Rose cite the example of people who, having migrated some fifteen miles *within* the city boundaries of Glasgow or Birmingham, were not eligible; on the other hand, people who had moved 'a few hundred yards over a district council boundary' were permitted a postal vote. Other voices were raised in protest against this anomaly, and it was referred to by the Labour Party's opening spokesman in the debate of 21st July 1960 on Political Expenditure (Control).

(iii) *Broadcasting and Television*: The significance of sound broad-casting and of television in the 1959 General Election has been mentioned above, and has been ably dealt with by Butler and Rose.[80] That significance will almost surely increase. Hence, the case for reviewing electoral law to cope properly with the advent of these new forces will also grow stronger.[81]

Conclusions

The most important, persistent questions of reform in the field of elections and representation have for a long time been those of the voting system, the selection of candidates, and election expenses. Another problem which, whilst by no means new, has become increasingly urgent over recent years is that of the relationship between a Member and his constituents—and especially his local association. The exercise of his independent judgement by a Member has to be balanced by his consciousness of the views of those whom he represents. The relationship may become an impossible one without give-and-take on both sides. A Member can no longer expect the support of those who elected him if he departs frequently and seriously from their views; at the same time, the electors may be called upon to recognize that a Member has not only the interests and opinions of his constituents to consider, but also his judgement of the national interest and the dictates of his conscience. The problem is not made any simpler by the difficulty, or even the impossibility, of framing precise remedies. The 'give-and-take on both sides' referred to above seems the one practical answer.

Elections are the threshold to the whole mansion of parliamentary activity proper. Proposals for reform in this latter domain now fall to be considered.

NOTES AND REFERENCES

[1] D. E. Butler and R. Rose: *The British General Election of 1959*, Chap. VII: Television and Radio.

[2] Lord Eustace Cecil's objections to the 1867 Reform Bill are a good example. He is reported as saying that 'the Bill would perpetuate bribery and lead to an extension of the influence of wealth, *and eventually lead to manhood suffrage and electoral districts*'. (Parl. Deb. 3rd Series, Vol. CLXXXVIII, c. 595.)

[3] A reduction to eighteen had already been rejected (though not unanimously) by the 1944 Speaker's Conference. Lord Altrincham has suggested that the minimum age should be sixteen (*Manchester Guardian*, 27th October 1958, p. 12).

[4] Representation of the People Act, 1949 (Amendment) Bill. Second Reading, H.C. Deb. 617, cs. 1607-73, 19th February 1960.

[5] H.C. Deb. 617, c. 1634.

[6] Butler: *The Electoral System in Britain 1918-51*, 1953, p. 139.

[7] H.C. Deb. 507, c. 1861.

[8] Established under the House of Commons (Redistribution of Seats) Act of 1944, these Commissions have had their statutory duties subsequently amended in 1946 and 1948, consolidated in 1949, and further amended under the House of Commons (Redistribution of Seats) Act, 1958. For details of this whole question see: (i) Butler: *op. cit.*, and an article by that writer on 'The Redistribution of Seats', in *Public Administration*, Vol. 33, pp. 125-47; (ii) Richards: *Honourable Members: A Study of the British Backbencher*, pp. 45-9.

[9] Thus, the electorate of Caithness and Sutherland at the 1959 General Election totalled 26,716—compared with electorates of (for example) 72,441 and 68,209 at Hull East and Bournemouth West respectively.

[10] *Elections and Electors. Studies in Democratic Representation*, 1955, pp. 104-05.

[11] H.C. Deb. 470, cs. 1873-4. Mr. Davies wanted a Royal Commission to be set up to investigate the possibilities of colonial representation at Westminster.

[12] Ross: *op. cit.* Part V, Chaps. 18-22.
Mackay: *Coupon or Free?*, 1943, pp. 54-86.
Butler: *op. cit.* Part I.

[13] Ross, pp. 305-6.

[14] *ibid.* p. 321.

[15] Butler in *op. cit.* pp. 62-8 discusses the 'bargain' made with the Liberals.

[16] H.C. Deb. 283, c. 1746.

[17] *Op. cit.* p. 102. (Labour's victory in 1945 was secured with only 48% of the votes.)

[18] Preface to *Voting in Democracies* by E. Lakeman and J. D. Lambert, 1955, p. 9.

[19] The present system of a simple majority in single-member constituencies is described by Ross and by Lakeman and Lambert, where its failings and inequalities are noted at length.

[20] cf. the example cited by Richards, *op. cit.* p. 35, of the 1929 General Election result at Northwich: Lord C. Crichton-Stuart (C.) 15,477 (Elected); Mrs. B. A. Gould (Lab.) 15,473; J. D. Barlow (Lib.) 14,161.

[21] *The Contemporary Review*, Vol. CXLI, March 1932, pp. 296-308.

[22] cf. Grimond: *The New Liberal Democracy*, 1958, pp. 4-5; and G. Watson: *The Unservile State: Essays in Liberty and Welfare*, 1957, pp. 50-1.

[23] There are frequent remarks to that effect in the writer's *Elections and Electors*.

[24] Ross: *The Achievements of Representative Democracy*, 1952, p. 19.

[25] Lakeman and Lambert, pp. 132–48; also J. H. Humphreys: *Objections to P.R. Answered*, P.R. Society Pamphlet, No. 83.

[26] Amery: *Thoughts on the Constitution*, 1947, p. 55.

[27] Muir: *How Britain is Governed: A Critical Analysis of Modern Developments in the British System of Government*, 2nd ed. 1930, p. 181.

[28] cf. S. R. Brett in the *Quarterly Review*, Vol. 284, 1946, pp. 457–68.

[29] See: Preface to Lakeman and Lambert, p. 10. The question of the need or otherwise for 'strong government' crops up in a great many aspects of parliamentary reform: cf. Chaps. IV & V.

[30] *The Economist*, 10th June 1944, pp. 773–4.

[31] *Political Quarterly*, Vol. XV, 1944, pp. 113–23.

[32] cf. Harley in *Fortnightly Review*, September 1930, pp. 307–18.

[33] *The Independent Member of Parliament*, Hansard Society Pamphlet No. 2, 1946, p. 18.

[34] Laski, p. 53.

[35] Stewart: *The British Approach to Politics*, revised 3rd ed. 1955, p. 132.

[36] Bulmer-Thomas: *The Party System in Great Britain*, 1953, pp. 103–4. This latter objection is not admitted by Lakeman and Lambert: *op. cit.* pp. 132–4.

[37] Curtis: *Central Government: An Introduction*, 1956, p. 17.

[38] Lakeman and Lambert, p. 156.

[39] *ibid.*, p. 156. No attempt has been made to describe methods of proportional representation: these are discussed at length in Ross's books and in Lakeman and Lambert. Neither has the present brief summary of the arguments for and against proportional representation any claim to completeness. Readers wishing to study this very complex problem are referred to *Voting in Democracies*, and to the works by Mackay and Ross listed in the bibliography of this book.

[40] Very briefly, this system would ensure that the successful candidate in a single-member constituency had a majority of the votes polled. Candidates are placed by the voter in order of preference: if an absolute majority does not accrue to any candidate following the count of first preferences, the first preferences given for the lowest candidate are ignored and the second preferences of those voters are then distributed amongst the remaining candidates.

[41] *Manchester Guardian*, 8th March 1950, p. 6.

[42] *The Economist*, 6th December 1952, pp. 663–4. Another article appeared in the issue of 8th March 1958, pp. 824–5.

[43] At the 1959 General Election, the Conservatives regained the Torrington seat.

[44] Lakeman and Lambert also refer to this feature of the A.V. in *op. cit.* p. 65. Nigel Nicolson did not stand as a candidate at the 1959 General Election.

[45] *Manchester Guardian*, 31st March 1958, p. 6.

[46] *The Times*, 22nd May 1958, p. 11.

[47] *The Times*, 9th June 1958, p. 11.

[48] Lakeman and Lambert, *op. cit.* pp. 62–7.

[49] H.C. Deb. 253, c. 106.

[50] Lakeman and Lambert, pp. 66–7.

[51] *op. cit.* p. 188, Table 36.

[52] *ibid.* pp. 189–91.

[53] *ibid.* p. 190.

[54] Article in *The Times*, 27th January 1953, p. 9.

[55] H.C. Deb. 472, cs. 143-4.
[56] H.C. Deb. 531, c. 233.
[57] Hollis: *Can Parliament Survive?* 1949, p. 120.
[58] Amery, pp. 64-7; and H.C. Deb. 249, cs. 656 ff.
[59] Stewart, pp. 133-4. 'Functional Devolution' is discussed in section (b) of the following chapter.
[60] *The People and the Constitution*, 1956, pp. 297-302.
[61] *ibid.*, pp. 302-4; pp. 315-6; Gordon, pp. 163-4.
[62] *ibid.* p. 123.
[63] *The Economist*, 10th June 1944, pp. 773-4.
[64] *Encounter*, February 1955, pp. 12-20.
[65] *Listener*, 17th February 1932, pp. 236-7.
[66] 'The Member and His Constituency', Ramsay Muir Memorial Lecture, 1957.
[67] N. Nicolson, p. 43.
[68] Bulmer-Thomas, pp. 204 ff.
[69] *Some Proposals for Constitutional Reform: being the recommendations of a Group of Conservatives*, 1946, p. 39.
[70] *op. cit.* pp. 203 ff.
[71] *ibid.* pp. 228-31. (William Gallacher urged the abolition of the deposit, and its replacement by nomination papers carrying 150 signatures in a debate on 1st February 1944: H.C. Deb. 396, c. 1333.)
[72] *op. cit.* pp. 231-3.
[73] *Parliamentary Representation*, 1948, 2nd (enlarged) edition, pp. 230-1.
[74] The third Speaker's Conference expressed disapproval of direct or indirect payment of substantial sums to party organizations with a view to influencing such organizations in the choice of candidates.
[75] In a letter to *The Times* of 13th May 1958, J. A. Gillison stated that 'a union frequently pays 80 per cent of its candidate's election expenses and also some hundreds a year into the local party so long as its candidate remains the representative.... If Parliamentary government is to be respected, or, possibly, to survive, objective examination of this system of "tied" M.P.s is an urgent task'.
[76] *Elections and Electors*, pp. 290-1. The much broader question of the control of political expenditure, by parties and other interested organizations, is discussed in Chap. IV.
[77] H.C. Deb. 594, c. 967 (P. Gordon Walker). During this debate, the wider questions of political expenditure and of the publication of political parties' accounts were raised: refer, in this matter to Chapter IV.
[78] *The British General Election of 1959*, p. 141.
[79] *ibid.* pp. 142-3.
[80] *op. cit.* Chap. VII.
[81] cf. 'The Hand of the Law', in Granada TV's report on its *Election Marathon, 1959*, pp. 9ff., for an idea of the complex, confusing issues involved. It is too early to say as yet whether the Committee of Inquiry on Sound and Television Broadcasting, set up by the Postmaster-General in July 1960, will go some way towards meeting the demand for a review of existing law.

II

Devolution

(*a*) THE CASE FOR DEVOLUTION

It is a commonplace of criticism of Parliament that the House of Commons tries to do too much. Congestion follows, and, as a result, it is said that the Cabinet is taxed beyond its capacity for thinking and taking decisive action, that Ministers rely on their officials more and more, and that the outcome is the growth of bureaucracy. In addition, the House of Commons cannot deal with a tenth of the subjects which enthusiastic Members wish to raise, and the Members consequently become demoralized.[1] Critics of this state of affairs all seek for a way in which Parliament can be relieved of the distracting multiplicity of minor matters; the answer some of them suggest is a devolution of certain of Parliament's powers.[2]

Other people approach the idea of devolution from a different direction. Muir thought it could be argued that there was at present an excessive centralization of government, and that for this reason there should be some devolution;[3] only by setting up subsidiary Parliaments, said Lady Megan Lloyd George,[4] can the national affairs of Wales, Scotland and England be properly handled. Devolution of this kind would clearly help to foster national sentiment within the United Kingdom, said Laski.[5] Sometimes this latter plea for national devolution is coupled with the argument that it would make the central Parliament more capable of doing its work efficiently; but it is also sometimes advanced as being strong enough to stand on its own. Thus Ramsay MacDonald said he favoured devolution to subordinate national bodies, not on the ground of saving time in the House of Commons, but as a point of principle.[6]

For Notes and References see pages 39–41

27

A different reason for devolution was advanced by Christopher Hollis.[7] He believed it was the essence of democracy that everyone should do a little politics, and no one should do very much; the political butter, as it were, should be spread more thinly. Members of Parliament should do less political work than they do now, while the man whose only political action is to mark a ballot paper every five years or so, should do more. To achieve this end, much more work should be delegated from Westminster to subsidiary democratic bodies.

It is also frequently said that, with the increasing work on technical subjects that is nowadays undertaken by Parliament, there is a great deal of discussion on matters which many Members today cannot fully understand.[8] One answer to this could be that the discussion of such matters should devolve upon bodies of technical experts.

The supporters of devolution are able to cite the success it has achieved in various foreign countries and especially—as is most relevant—in the Northern Ireland Parliament.[9] Others point out that the powers given to the Church Assembly to initiate legislation have worked excellently.[10] These examples show the kind of thing that can be achieved by devolution, and suggest the moral that Parliament can solve its problems by giving away some limited powers to bodies other than itself.

From the reasons advanced in favour of devolution, it can be seen that its proponents tend to fall into two schools: those who think that subordinate bodies should be created in order to range over a certain area of national administration—such as agriculture, or industry—and those who believe that devolution should start geographically, that certain areas should be allowed their own super-local government. These two types of devolution—'Functional' and 'Regional'—now fall to be considered.

(b) FUNCTIONAL DEVOLUTION

Sir Richard Acland suggested that the House of Commons should be divided into two halves—one, the 'Supreme Council of State', to deal with the more important matters, and the other, the 'Council for Minor Matters', which would deal with the rest.

Members should be allowed to have deputies, and it would be the deputies who would normally sit in the second Council.[11]

The creation of subordinate assemblies, which could bring expert opinion to bear on proposed new legislation, has been put forward at various times. The idea has, of course, affinities with other schemes which suggest the creation of specialist Committees of Members of Parliament for this purpose. But these other schemes—which are based on the existing framework of Parliament —are discussed elsewhere.[12]

Lord Eustace Percy suggested in 1931 that an advisory Assembly of interested parties could usefully be created in order to assist in preparing legislation dealing with economic matters, and legislation affecting local authorities. If such an Assembly were to register its agreement to a proposed new bill, the House would then be able to deal summarily with it.[13]

Something along these lines was also suggested by R. D. Denman, who was more specific about the legislative procedure to be used. Specialist assemblies should be set up to initiate legislation, which would then proceed in the same manner as Church Assembly Measures.[14] He suggested that agriculture, transport, social insurance and housing could all devolve in this way upon subordinate assemblies; perhaps transport would be the best beginning—it was a technical subject, it needed more attention than the House could give it, and (writing in 1933) he said it excited no strong party animus.[15] As a result, he suggested on another occasion, 'a specialist Assembly, given work by this House or originating work of their own, rationed as to finance by this House, submitting to us their conclusions for acceptance or rejection, would make once more possible that this House should be an efficient legislative machine.'[16]

W. G. S. Adams suggested that the great departments of state— such as the Board of Trade and the Ministry of Agriculture— should set up councils representative of the interests which they administer; such councils would initiate much of our social and economic legislation. Parliament would then to some extent be relieved of the need to discuss such measures—for they would already have been discussed publicly—and could concentrate its attention on the effects of the measures on the community at large, and on the financial obligations involved.[17]

The various Assemblies and Councils considered above have been concerned entirely with the legislative side of Parliament's function. Other, broader, proposals have been made to create Assemblies which, while including legislation among their duties, have wider powers—powers which, in some respects, can rival those of either House of Parliament. The three most considered schemes of this kind are those put forward by the Webbs (in 1920), by Winston Churchill (1930), and by Hollis (1949).

Political and Social Co-Parliaments

The Webbs' plan to divide Parliament's functions into two, and to have a social Parliament co-existing with a political one, was published in 1920.[18] It was re-stated by Mrs. Webb in an article in 1931,[19] and has been so discussed by later writers that it can usefully be reconsidered here.

A new National Assembly, of about 300 members from England and Wales, and fifty from Scotland, would be directly elected on the same franchise as the House of Commons, for a fixed period —say three years. Groups of statutes would be referred to the Assembly, which would be allowed to make regulations under them (much as Ministers now make statutory instruments). The services which would in this way devolve upon the Assembly would be health, education, labour, agriculture and fisheries, transport, mines, works, and some of those which are at present administered by the Home Office and the Board of Trade. Private Bill legislation would also fall to the Assembly.

Finance, as Mrs. Webb admitted in her article of 1931, is the biggest puzzle in any scheme of devolution. The National Assembly should have its own revenue; but on the whole it would be more of a supervising than a spending authority, and the House of Commons would continue to be responsible for the national debt, defence, war pensions, the Post Office, justice, prisons and the colonies. Revenue for those services controlled by the Assembly would come from the devolution of existing taxes, or by precepts to local authorities, or by new forms of taxation. The Assembly's procedure would be based, not on that of the House of Commons, but on that of local authorities. The system of administration by

Committees would enable all members to participate in government, and would ensure closer control.

There would be plenty of work left to the House of Commons —in fact 'all the functions of government known to Pitt and Canning, to Peel and Palmerston, and even to Gladstone and Disraeli prior to the seventies'.[20]

Summing up, Mrs. Webb said that her scheme recognized a clear distinction in the functions of government. On the one hand, there were sovereignty, foreign affairs, defence, law, justice—all functions based on the exercise of power; on the other there were the social services in all their forms—subjects for organized co-operation among citizens. To mix the issues arising out of these two functions was illogical and confusing, for an elector might be an internationalist and pacifist in foreign affairs *and* a believer in private enterprise in social affairs; he may believe in a national health service *and* be an imperialist.

Mrs. Webb's scheme could, she said, be adapted for regional devolution as well; there might be Assemblies for England, Scotland and Wales, which would administer common services by a series of joint committees, or by joint meetings of all the Assemblies. But, preferably, the one Assembly would cover the whole of Great Britain.

The Economic Sub-Parliament

In the Romanes lecture of 1930, Winston Churchill said that the great change that had come over Parliament since the first world war was its new preoccupation with economics; and this presented a dangerous new challenge to its survival. As a remedy, he suggested the creation of an economic sub-Parliament of non-political, non-partisan experts, about a fifth of the size of the present Commons and chosen by it.[21]

These general proposals were elaborated and modified by Churchill in the evidence he gave before the Select Committee on Procedure.[22] The sub-Parliament would, he said, consist of forty M.P.s and eighty others—twenty of them peers, the rest being businessmen, Trades Union representatives and economic experts. They would all be chosen to reflect party strengths in the House of Commons, and would serve a three-year period of membership (which period would not be affected by a general election).

All trade and industry bills would be referred to this body, unless the House of Commons otherwise decided. Other bills—or parts of other bills—could, if the House so resolved, also be sent for its consideration. These bills would eventually be returned to the House of Commons with the criticisms and recommendations of the sub-Parliament. The Economic sub-Parliament could also, if it so wished, initiate inquiries into questions of economic importance, and report its findings to both Houses of Parliament. The expected effect of this arrangement would be to provide a forum where important economic questions could be discussed in a dispassionate non-party atmosphere.

This plan excited considerable interest and controversy, and is still considered from time to time. In 1931, Samuel thought it impracticable,[23] but as re-stated by Amery (who stressed that the Commons would remain the dominant element in the legislature),[24] it has been advocated by Harold Macmillan.[25]

Industrial Legislatures

J. H. Harley, in 1930, suggested that proposed industrial legislation should be allotted to a functional Parliament, at least for preliminary consideration. This Parliament—modelled on the German Supreme Economic Council of the time—would remain subordinate to the national Parliament, which would continue to regulate the industrial policy of the future; but this policy itself could only succeed if it was prefaced by mutual discussion and agreement between the organized bodies of masters and men.[26] Other people have advocated industrial parliaments along the same lines; thus Kenworthy, in 1931, favoured the setting up of such a Parliament, which would consist of representatives of employers and employees.[27]

But the scheme of this kind which has attracted most attention in the recent past has been that put forward by Hollis in 1949.[28] This proposed a third parliamentary chamber, the 'House of Industry', consisting of Members elected, not—as in Churchill's suggestion—by the political Parliament, but by direct election from 'occupational constituencies' of industrial workers.[29]

This new House would have definite legislative responsibilities, modelled on those of the Church Assembly; it '. . . should play in industrial affairs the part which the Church Assembly plays in ecclesiastical affairs'. It would pass legislation on technical matters and submit it for the approval or otherwise of the House of Commons. Hollis's views have been echoed most recently by Sir Henry Legge-Bourke, who believed that the creation of an Industrial House would result in a closer examination of the great annual sums of money spent on the national industries.[30]

(c) CRITICISMS OF FUNCTIONAL DEVOLUTION

The Webbs' proposal has aroused a certain amount of opposition; Muir called it 'unworkable'—a frequent epithet for schemes of devolution—and Laski thought it would prove difficult in practice to decide into which category, political or social, a particular matter fell.[31] Furthermore, the Webbs' proposal—like Churchill's—could lead to a state of affairs in which the two parliaments were of different political complexions.[32] Jennings said that a government must have unified control over affairs; yet, since foreign affairs and trade policy fell to be decided by different parliaments, the electorate might be able to vote for foreign and economic policies which were quite incompatible.[33]

Laski criticized Hollis's proposal on the ground that the basis of industrial representation had not been sufficiently explained. Were Labour and Capital interests to be weighted equally? Was the housewife to be represented? It was probable that some distinctive industries might prove too small to warrant a constituency of their own; would they have to be joined together? And how was the consumers' interest to be safeguarded?[34]

Curtis, while agreeing that functional devolution would result in a better representation of industrial and similar 'occupational' interests, in a more experienced appraisal of matters of that kind, and in an avoidance of the hampering discipline of the political parties, listed six points of weakness or danger in such a system.[35] These were: (1) There was the possibility of conflict between the two Parliaments. This could only be avoided by making the new Parliament purely advisory: and in that case the supreme Parliament could always ignore its proposals. (2) If it was attempted to make the new Parliament powerful, the present Parliament could always override it by virtue of its ultimate financial control. (3) The division of functions between the two parliamentary bodies would prove difficult to define. (4) The method of election of Members for the new body would present difficulties. (5) Experts cannot be expected to show expertise over all the subjects which the new body will discuss; in part of the discussions, they would only be able to put forward the views of an amateur. (6) The experience of continental countries, possessing similar Councils, shows that it is very difficult to avoid party alignments.

On the other hand Lord (formerly Sir Gilbert) Campion, in considering the suggested ways of increasing Parliament's effectiveness, thought that functional devolution might do this. He believed Churchill's sub-Parliament to be more promising than the Webbs' co-Parliament.[36]

(d) REGIONAL DEVOLUTION

The demands for devolution of this kind are not always put forward as an alternative to schemes of functional devolution; the two are often proposed together. As mentioned above, Mrs. Webb, in her scheme for a social co-Parliament, went to some length to show it could be adopted to meet the demands of those who wanted a measure of regional autonomy; Churchill, while he was putting forward his scheme of an economic sub-Parliament, also favoured 'very considerable changes in the direction of devolution to local bodies much larger in scale than any that exist, or almost any that exist, in the country at the present time'.[37]

Regional devolution is advocated for a mixture of reasons; partly it is proposed as a more efficient system of government, partly as a way of relieving Parliament of its present great load of business, and partly as a means of satisfying or fostering local loyalties.

Lord Samuel started from the premise that Parliament was giving inadequate attention to many of the subjects under its control; and the only thorough remedy for this was the devolution of business to subordinate legislatures and ministries.[38] Devolution should be geographical, not functional; in addition to the examples provided by many foreign and commonwealth countries, Northern

Ireland shows how it could work. The obvious next steps were to provide Assemblies for Scotland and Wales, followed possibly by Northern and Southern England Assemblies. In an article in *Crossbow*, Adams has recently pointed to a malaise in Scottish public life, caused by dissatisfaction at the way the Scottish Office deals with Scottish affairs. The suggested answer to this situation was to set up a second House of Lords in Edinburgh, where Scottish peers would perform the functions *vis-à-vis* Scottish legislation, etc. which the Upper House at present performs at Westminster. Adams also thought that the Parliament at Westminster should be relieved of the domestic affairs of the different countries in the United Kingdom; devolution of this kind was essential.[39] The regional parliaments would probably not require second chambers. The central parliament could then be reduced in size.

Muir thought that Parliament was not only under too much strain, but that government was also over-centralized. He was inclined to believe that regional devolution provided the answer, and suggested the setting-up of regional authorities for Scotland, Wales, and seven areas in England.[40]

The demands for Scottish and Welsh Home Rule seem to spring from grounds of national pride, rather than from the intention of making the present Parliament more effective: though occasionally the two reasons are coupled together, as when Lady Megan Lloyd George advanced them both to favour Parliaments of Wales and Scotland on the Northern Ireland model.[41] Powers to be transferred to the regional Parliaments would include agriculture, fisheries, forestry, education, health and housing. Reserved for the central Parliament would be its powers in connexion with the Crown, foreign and commonwealth affairs, defence, customs and tariffs. Powers relating to coinage, postal services, docks, harbours and electoral law would be shared.

This system, as far as Wales was concerned, had been set out in a pamphlet published in 1953,[42] and was to be repeated in an unsuccessful Private Member's Bill that came before the House of Commons in 1955.[43] It is too early yet to say what long-term effects the creation of a Minister for Welsh Affairs in 1951 may have on the demands for Welsh autonomy; but from recent events, it does not seem that those demands have been stilled.[44]

35

Lady Megan's father had been a supporter of regional devolution, thinking it especially relevant to the needs of a community as big as London.[45] The Liberal Party has continued to advocate it; a manifesto issued at the time of the 1959 General Election offered Scottish and Welsh Parliaments on the lines advocated by Lady Megan.[46] As an immediate step, they said, Wales should have its own Secretary of State in the Cabinet.[47]

(e) CRITICISMS OF REGIONAL DEVOLUTION

Jennings thought that Muir, in inclining towards regional devolution, had omitted to consider two problems: what were the subjects to be devolved, and what were to be the financial relations between the central and regional parliaments? In any case, the relief to Parliament would not be great: England was a single economic unit, and the co-ordinating legislation—which would thus be necessary in respect of each devolved subject—would take up all the 'saved' time. Even if powers were devolved only to Scotland and Wales, the time saved would not be worth the cost and complication involved.[48]

R. J. Lawrence attacked the very citadel of regional devolution on two fronts by saying that, in any area other than Northern Ireland, a separate legislature would aggravate rather than mollify social conflict; and that the supposed benefits of devolution to Northern Ireland had not been as great as generally believed.[49] The problem was basically a financial and economic one. Devolution presumed that the United Kingdom was to remain united, and it follows from this that certain conditions must govern the relations between the constituent countries: no area must be able to discriminate against the others, and all areas must share the benefits and contribute to the cost of the common services. Hence, fiscal policies must be uniform, and taxation as well as social services must be substantially uniform, in order to prevent the flow of persons, goods and capital from one area to another. There would consequently be almost no scope for independent action in administration or policy; it would be both difficult and unwise for a subordinate parliament to act independently except in a few minor matters.

Lawrence supported his argument by an examination of the

relationship between Northern Ireland and the rest of the United Kingdom; most Northern Ireland legislation simply re-enacted that passed at Westminster. Devolution was accordingly unlikely to confer on Scotland and Wales advantages that could not be secured in simpler ways, and might well create new difficulties in those areas by stirring up rivalries and conflicts.

These arguments were countered by A. H. Birch, who argued that Lawrence was wrong in basing his arguments against devolution on the experience of Northern Ireland, because that country had never done what the advocates of devolution had wanted her to—namely, initiate legislation that differed from the British Acts.[50] There was no reason why Parliaments for Scotland and Wales should not do this. But they would need greater financial powers so that they could finance some services by local taxation; their level of services would depend on how much revenue they could raise without injuring their economic position. It was not true to say that differences in tax rates would harm the whole nation's economy; it had not done so in America. Federalism was generally stimulating to the economy precisely because it promoted mobility of capital and labour, and the consequent location of resources in the area in which their productivity was greatest.

But perhaps Laski and Hollis have expressed most succinctly the practical views of the critics of regional devolution—Laski, when he said that the basic economic unity of Great Britain prevented any effective devolution,[51] and Hollis when he claimed that Home Rule for Scotland and Wales would not noticeably reduce the burden on the central government, since they were all so much part of the British industrial system.[52] So far as Scotland alone is concerned, the last word may be sought in the Royal Commission which reported in 1954. Much of the pressure for Home Rule came, they thought, from an ignorance of the extent to which devolution of Scottish affairs had already taken place.[53]

(f) OTHER KINDS OF DEVOLUTION

Jennings mentions the possibility of granting more legislative powers direct to Ministers as a sort of devolution; but he adds that this is not a form which generally commends itself to the advocates of devolution.[54] He suggests, however, one way in which it might be considered: all private bills could be controlled directly by Departments, rather than, as at present, having to go through the legislative procedure of both Houses.

Other critics have suggested that the sphere of action of local authorities could usefully be enlarged;[55] Salter, for instance, believed that more actual responsibility for policy should be given to them.[56] But Jennings thought that the time Parliament could save by this means would be 'almost infinitesimal', and that there was, in any case, very little that could be devolved in this way.[57]

Conclusion

Each new proposed scheme of devolution has to face two questions—will it work, and will it help?

The practicability of each new scheme is always attacked. Perhaps it is for this reason that the believers in devolution tend to be content with broad general statements of their aims, rather than give details which may be vulnerable and unpopular. By doing so, they leave themselves open to the rebuke of the 1931/2 Select Committee on Procedure: 'These proposals seem ... to have been inadequately considered.'[58] However, the fact that devolution is, in some forms and in some circumstances, practicable, can be inferred from its existing successes in Northern Ireland and in the Church Assembly.

The second question—Will it help?—is apt to draw different answers from different people, since they are considering different ends; some think devolution should aim to help Parliament, while others believe its purpose should be to help those regions (or interests) on whom the powers devolve. It is this mixture of motives which clouds the glass. If the question means, 'Will devolution help the natural aspirations of the regions within Great Britain?' the answer is clearly 'Yes, if such aspirations exist'; but regionalization has its drawbacks, as *Passport to Pimlico* showed. If the question means, 'Will devolution help Parliament?' the answer is in doubt; it seems superficially probable, but Baldwin said it would in fact create more work in the long run, and several writers have agreed with him.[59] If, finally, it is asked, 'Will devolution help the country at large by bringing together a body who can give expert appraisal to technical matters in a national, non-political way?' the answer

would seem to be that it is a consummation devoutly to be wished;
but that the practical difficulties of creating such a body, and
defining both its powers and its relationship to the House of
Commons, are formidable.

One thing is reasonably sure: if regional devolution comes, it
will come only as a result of a spontaneous and widespread demand
for it from the regions concerned.[60] It will come from below, and
not from on top; for, as Denman pointed out, devolution is never
popular among M.P.s, who prefer to try to handle everything
themselves.[61]

However, with the mounting complexity and increasing congestion of parliamentary life, it may be that Parliament will eventually
take a half-step towards devolution by setting up committees of
Members who will specialize in certain areas of administration,
and keep the House informed of what they find out. In this respect,
the recent creation of a Welsh Grand Committee and the extended
functions of the Scottish Grand Committee (both of which now
hold general debates on the problems of their countries) might be
significant. A further change along these lines would not, of course,
be devolution. Parliament would be retaining all its powers, but
would be using them in a different way—and proposals of this
kind are considered in Chapter III. However, being either regional
or functional, such committees might to some small extent fulfil
the expectations which advocates of devolution claim for their own
schemes. If one then went on to allow for joint meetings of two
or more of these committees, one would perhaps be advancing
towards 'that subsidiary or collateral assembly' which is the goal
of devolution.[62]

NOTES AND REFERENCES

[1] e.g. Mrs. Sidney Webb: 'A Reform Bill for 1932' in *Political Quarterly*,
Vol. II, 1931, pp. 1–22.
[2] R. D. Denman: *Nineteenth Century and After*, Vol. 113, January 1933,
pp. 74–9.
[3] Muir: *How Britain is Governed*, 2nd ed. 1930, p. 282.
[4] *Parliamentary Reform*, Vol. VIII, 1954–5.
[5] Laski, p. 46.
[6] H.C. 161 of 1930/1, Q. 14–5.
[7] *Manchester Guardian*, 13th November 1952.
[8] e.g. H.C. Deb. 510 cs. 564–5.
[9] see Sir Herbert Samuel: *Political Quarterly*, Vol. II, 1931, pp. 309–12.

D

[10] Denman, *art. cit.*, pp. 76–7.

[11] Acland: *What It Will be Like in the New Britain*, 1942, p. 170.

[12] See the following chapter on Procedure.

[13] H.C. 161 of 1930/1, Q. 1964.

[14] Under the Church of England Assembly (Powers) Act, 1919, the Church Assembly can propose legislation 'touching matters concerning the Church of England'. Such 'Measures' are considered by the Ecclesiastical Committee (a Joint Committee of fifteen members from each House, chosen by the Lord Chancellor and the Speaker). This Committee cannot amend the Measure, but makes a report stating the effect of it, and its views on its expediency. Each House considers this report and votes to accept or reject the Measure (without amendment). On a single affirmative decision from each House, the Measure is presented for the Royal Assent, and becomes law.

[15] Denman: *art. cit.*

[16] H.C. Deb. 260, cs. 2162–3.

[17] *Listener*, 17th February 1933, p. 236.

[18] *A Constitution for the Socialist Commonwealth of Great Britain.*

[19] *Political Quarterly*, Vol. II, 1931, pp. 1–22.

[20] Mrs. Sidney Webb: *art. cit.* p. 20.

[21] Romanes lecture, 19th June 1930. O.U.P. 1930.

[22] H.C. 161 of 1930/1, Q. 3750 ff.

[23] He was arguing in favour of regional devolution: *art. cit.* p. 310.

[24] Amery: *Thoughts on the Constitution*, 1947, p. 67.

[25] In a speech at Brighton, 5th March 1949.

[26] *Fortnightly Review*, Vol. 128, New Series, September 1930.

[27] H.C. 161 of 1930/1, Q. 3139.

[28] Hollis: *Can Parliament Survive?*, Chap. IX.

[29] 'Functional representation' (see section (*h*) of Chap. I) had been called for by Amery, p. 65, who had suggested applying it to Churchill's scheme for an Economic sub-Parliament.

[30] H.C. Deb. 619, cs. 1356–7.

[31] Muir, p. 296.

[32] Laski, p. 48.

[33] Jennings: *Parliamentary Reform*, 1934, pp. 53–5.

[34] Laski, pp. 48–9.

[35] Curtis, pp. 45 ff.

[36] Lord Campion and others: *Parliament: A Survey*, 1952, p. 32.

[37] H.C. 161 of 1930/1, Q. 1513.

[38] *art. cit.* p. 309.

[39] Adams: *Crossbow*, Vol. 4, No. 10, p. 8.

[40] Muir, Chapter VIII.

[41] *Parliamentary Affairs*, Vol. VIII, No. 4, 1955.

[42] *Parliament for Wales*, Aberystwyth 1953.

[43] H.C. Bill 21 of 1955: H.C. Deb., 537, cs. 2439–527.

[44] See *Manchester Guardian*, 12th December 1958.

[45] H.C. 161 of 1930/1, Q. 459.

[46] See Motion, 15th December 1952; and *The Unservile State: Essays in Liberty and Welfare*, edited by G. Watson, 1957, pp. 51–2.

[47] *People Count*, published by the Liberal Party, 1959.

[48] Jennings, *op. cit.*, pp. 45–7.

[49] 'Devolution Reconsidered' in *Political Studies*, Vol. IV, 1956, pp. 1–17.

[50] *Political Studies*, Vol. IV, 1956, pp. 310–11.

[51] Laski, pp. 46–7.
[52] Hollis, p. 79.
[53] Cmd. 9212, para 30.
[54] Jennings, *op. cit.*, pp. 37, 40.
[55] Adams: *art. cit.*
[56] Lord Campion and others, Chap. V.
[57] Jennings, *op. cit.*, p. 41.
[58] H.C. 129 of 1931/2, para. 4.
[59] H.C. 161 of 1930/1, Q. 212.
[60] Lord Samuel: *art. cit.* p. 312.
[61] Denman: *art. cit.*
[62] Lord Campion and others, Chap. XIII.

III

Procedure

'Procedure is all the constitution the poor Briton has.' This observation by Sir Kenneth Pickthorn, during the debate on Procedure of 8th February 1960, underlines the importance of a subject which may not at first sight appear to afford much general interest.[1] A study of the subject must indeed start with the nature of Parliament itself, and, in the same debate, R. A. Butler gave his views on this: Parliament, to be healthy, must not only be a legislative assembly, and the arena in which the struggle for power takes place; it must also be a place that captures the popular imagination.[2]

Various writers have listed the functions which Parliament exists to perform; and these can be separated under the general headings of legislation, finance and deliberation. Parliamentary procedure, which can be defined as the internal arrangements each House makes for the carrying out of these functions, may in its turn be considered under those same headings—but with the general proviso that, just as the 'deliberative' function is to some extent implicit within both the others, that category will contain some procedural items (such as 'Divisions') which are common to all three.

It will be found that there is very little to say about procedural reform in the House of Lords. This might be said to show a certain complacency about the Lords' procedure—procedure which in some respects seems archaic, even by House of Commons standards. But the general satisfaction—or, at the least, the absence of dissatisfaction—is more probably based on the different conditions of life in the Lords: the less work to do (for there is no financial

For Notes and References see pages 86–94

business), the smaller numbers who attend (despite the greater total number), and perhaps the absence of those traditions of obstruction which the Commons have known. There may also be a feeling that, if the Commons find a certain major change in procedure desirable, the Lords—as the less potent of the Houses —will, in their own leisurely time, find it convenient to follow suit.

This chapter will, then, discuss proposals for procedural reform under the three headings—Financial Control; Legislative Control; and General Procedural Reforms, which will take in proposed reforms within the 'deliberative' functioning of the House of Commons, together with some other reforms which affect the performance of all its functions. Before considering these, however, we must look at certain suggestions which, in their entirety, would come nearest to providing a total reform of the House's procedure: we must examine the suggestions made for transforming the House's Committee system.

(a) THE SYSTEM OF COMMITTEES

In considering the many detailed schemes that have been put forward for parliamentary reform since about 1930, it is astonishing to find how widespread has been the belief that the House of Commons ought to set up specialized Committees of Members who would act as some form of link between the House and individual Departments of State. The reasons that are advanced in support of these Committees vary, as do the forms which it is suggested they should take; but it is clear that any scheme which, in general outline, has commanded support from such names as Acland, Amery, Campion, Cripps, Fellowes, Grimond, Hollis, Jennings, Laski, Muir, Salter and G. M. Young—among many others—is worthy of the closest attention.

The proposal to use specialized parliamentary Committees of this kind was much in the air in the 1920s and 1930s; there was considerable argument, especially within the Labour Party, on the point.[3] These arguments rather worked themselves to a standstill, but interest in the subject has revived in recent years, and it was one of the major reforms considered by the Select Committee on Procedure in 1958/9.

The reason behind this general proposal is not just the usual one that it would save parliamentary time; there is first the feeling that the whole question of Parliament's control over the Executive, the whole relationship between Whitehall and Westminster, needs to be re-appraised.[4] Underlying this conviction is the belief that Members of Parliament are no longer capable collectively of exercising control over some aspects of administration; in order to be able to do so, they should know more about a Department's working and the Minister's reasoning. Thus, in the early 1930s, Lord Ponsonby was complaining that Parliament no longer had any say in foreign affairs; only a Foreign Affairs Committee, which would provide close contact between the Foreign Secretary and Members, could re-establish the greatest safeguard for peace —which was parliamentary control of the Executive.[5] Specialized Committees were necessary, said Lloyd George in 1931, in order that Members should be able to get hold of all the information that was available to Ministers; the Committees would publish reports, which would be debated, and the House would be better informed.[6] Greaves thought that realistic and effective discussion of departmental activities would follow, if the House had the aid of these specialized Committees.[7] Lord Cottenham said that the whole principle of the Executive's responsibility to Parliament was in danger, and that the remedy was an impartial supervision of each Department's work by a Committee of M.P.s.[8] K. C. Wheare believed that informal, all-party Committees, covering the whole range of administrative activity, able to keep in touch with Minisers and to discuss matters with the Department concerned, would be the best way of controlling bureaucracy.[9] Peering into the future, Young thought that the main function of Parliament was going to lie in the control it exercised over the Executive, and that the easiest way of making this control effective lay in regular conferences between the Minister and his officials on the one hand, and Members of Parliament on the other.[10]

A system of this kind would clearly be objected to by Ministers, said Lloyd George, but he believed that it would do them and their officials good.[11] H. R. G. Greaves felt that the activities of a Committee of this kind would enhance the reputation of a good administrator.[12] Amery, speaking from his experience of office, thought such a Committee would actually have been a help to him.[13]

Lord Campion pointed out that advisory Committees of this kind need not controvert the basic tenet of the House's Committee system, which was that Committees should remain subordinate to the House.[14] Nor, said Brogan, need they upset the basis of our parliamentary government—that is, Cabinet control.[15] Both Lord Eustace Percy[16] and Lord Cottenham[17] thought that Parliament could, through a use of these Committees, act on that historic principle which had rather lost its effectiveness: 'the redress of grievances should precede supply'.

One great virtue of Committees like this was that policy and administration could be looked at in a dispassionate 'super-party' spirit, inside Parliament; both Lloyd George[18] and Lord Campion[19] underlined this point. Grimond said that it was difficult to deal with some major matters in the full blaze of political controversy, and that a use of Committees could obviate this. One of the most disturbing aspects of the Suez affray was that the Opposition was not consulted, and the House felt it was being kept deliberately and unnecessarily in the dark. Enlightenment could have been given in an all-party Committee, had one existed.[20] It has similarly been argued that the only way in which the welfare of a Colony can be considered by the House before an emergency there demands action (which might come too late), is by the existence of a specialist Committee which would meet regularly and keep the affairs of all Colonies constantly in mind.[21]

Adoption of this kind of Committee system would, it is said, make a great difference in the effectiveness of each individual Member's work in Parliament. Members would gain real knowledge of certain subjects,[22] and become truly effective in those spheres.[23] A former Speaker has said that 'departmental' Committees would certainly enable Members to acquire a better knowledge of how public money was spent,[24] and this would clearly be an advantage to them. Brogan argued that, from the examples of France and America, it could be seen that these Committees also gave Members greater experience of 'real'—that is, 'executive'—legislation.[25]

These Committees would, it was thought, provide a useful and important job for back-bench members who so often have little useful to do.[26] Members would feel that they were sharing in the effective work of Parliament,[27] and they could do so without—as

45

at present—sitting all day in the Chamber waiting to 'get in' with a speech.[28] Thus the role of Members would have restored to it not only reality, but also influence, said Salter;[29] and Jennings believed that if ever private Members were to do anything more than walk through the lobbies, a development of the Committee system and the process of specialization was essential.[30]

When the practicability of the scheme is called in question, its apologists have three answers: it works in foreign countries, it has to some minor extent already been successfully employed here, and the system it is designed to replace is in some respects clearly a less efficient weapon than this would prove to be.

Comparing the British with American and French parliamentary systems, Brogan averred that in those other countries there is more 'parliamentary government' than with us.[31] Taking a broader view, Lord Campion pointed out that most legislative bodies have recognized the need to organize themselves in this way, in order to cope with the complexities of modern state business: the House of Commons itself relied for leadership on its Select Committees in the seventeenth century.[32]

One British Committee which is cited as an example of how the system has already, to a small degree, been worked successfully here, is the Select Committee on National Expenditure which was set up during the war. The reports of this Committee, said R. S. W. Pollard,[33] show the sort of useful thing that can be expected from a specialized Committee.[34]

In 1932, Adams was citing the Estimates Committee as the progenitor of the kind of committee he wanted.[35] Sir Edward Fellowes thought that the sort of Committee that could emerge might resemble the Public Accounts Committee;[36] but a direct precedent was the Joint Committee on Indian Affairs that had done useful work in 1921 and 1922, when it had had wide general terms of reference.[37] A resemblance to the Scottish Grand Committee has also been pointed out.[38]

The aspect of the present parliamentary system which, it is claimed, could not fail to be improved by the adoption of the new system, is the work done now by Committees of the Whole House. Hollis has said that everyone agrees it to be a farce that a parliament of over 600 members should control the nation's business.[39] In the proposals he put before the Select Committee on Procedure in 1931, Jowett said that the House must completely abandon the practice of going into Committee of the Whole House, and leave the work to 'departmental' Committees instead.[40] Referring only to finance, Jennings thought that the Committees of Supply and Ways and Means were not competent to deal with points of detail, and should be superseded by a small Committee of Members who would soon become quasi-expert.[41]

Against the weight of all these arguments, the opposition has been more rare than might be expected and, on the whole, more guarded. The principle counter-argument has been that foreign experience of the successful working of these Committees is not relevant in Great Britain, since their legislatures are founded on the doctrine of the separation of powers between the legislature and the executive; Muir said that the American or French system could not be transplanted as it stood.[42] It was for this reason that Laski thought the U.S. Senate Committee on Foreign Relations was not an appropriate model for the Parliament at Westminster (though he went on to describe the kind of Committee which he thought could be useful),[43] and Campion was very careful to point out that the French system of *commissions permanentes*', which he was advocating, would need to be modified if it was to be adopted at Westminster.[44] The Select Committee on Procedure in 1958/59, rejecting by a small majority a proposal along these lines, described it as 'a radical constitutional innovation'.[45] Strachey and Joad protested against the proposed new system, because it would lead, they thought, to a complete fusion of Parliament and the Executive.[46] R. A. Butler has recently said it would get in the way of administration and blur ministerial responsibility.[47]

Of the other words said in criticism or qualification of the proposed change, Fitzroy pointed out that it would not, he thought, save any parliamentary time,[48] and Samuel was on the whole not convinced by the arguments put forward.[49] Lees-Smith went further. He believed that the existence of these Committees would kill the prospect of a Government with any driving power; Ministers would be driven to placate them and to compromise.[50]

But the most formidable of recent critics has been Herbert (now Lord) Morrison.[51] Referring to the American and French system of Committees, he said that Governments tend to become the 'victims or creatures of Committees'; our own Parliament, he continued, would regard the practice as a derogation of its authority. Referring to the Jowett (I.L.P.) proposals, he said they would make the life of the Minister almost intolerable; they might also embarrass the official Opposition, who might find themselves attacking a policy which had been endorsed by their Members on the Committee; and they would, finally, challenge the vital doctrine of the responsibility of Ministers to Parliament as a whole.

The General Functions of the Proposed Departmental Committees

We have seen that a wide range of opinion has held that Parliament should set up Committees which would each concern themselves with a particular field of government administration. Not unnaturally, opinions differ as to what would be the precise nature and functions of such Committees, and now we must turn to consider these. However, it should be pointed out that many writers—while they have been keen to stress the virtues of the idea—have not felt it necessary to argue for or against the details of how it would work out. They all envisage a fairly small Committee keeping an eye on each department, and thus being informed—and keeping the House informed—of the reasons on which policy decisions have been taken; but they have not all concerned themselves with the details of the form the Committee should take. Where such details have been mentioned, they draw attention to the kind of things that would have to be thought of if the Committees were established; but the weight of opinion for or against a particular point will not be reflected in the number of people who have gone on record in support or opposition of it, because so many of the proponents of the general idea have not expressed themselves on its resulting complications.

With this *caveat*, we can consider the details of the scheme. Some of the general questions to be decided are: Should the Committee have legislative duties? Should it control departmental expenditure? Should it control a department's delegated legislation? What departments are particularly in need of this kind of parliamentary control? A basic factor, which must be clearly defined, concerns the exact relationship between the Committee and the Minister. Finally, we can consider various detailed suggestions about the size, constitution, powers and terms of reference of the Committee.

Should the Committee Have Legislative Duties?

A number of those who advocate the setting-up of these departmental Committees contend that they are the appropriate bodies to take the Committee stage of bills affecting their departments. Others go further, and say the Committees should actually initiate legislation.[52]

Among those who favoured the idea of these Committees taking the Committee stage of relevant bills was Jennings. He had elsewhere advocated that Standing Committees, which take the Committee stage of bills, should be composed of specialists; and he thought it would be unnecessary duplication to have two different specialist committees dealing with the same subject-matter.[53] Jowett, speaking for the I.L.P., believed that the one Committee should consider all matters relating to a particular Department, and this would include the Committee stage of bills.[54] The Joint Committee on Indian Affairs (1921–29), which Fellowes suggested as a prototype for future Specialized Committees, included in its duties the examination of bills.[55] Hollis based his views on the procedure of the Parliament in Holland. There, each new bill is presented by the Minister to the relevant departmental Committee, and, together and in private, they go through it in detail. Only after this opportunity for feeling the way and for considering possible modifications is the bill debated publicly.[56]

Others have favoured the idea that these Committees should take more than just the Committee stage of each bill; Stafford Cripps, for instance, said they might themselves suggest legislation.[57] Pollard, who particularized very fully the functions of these Committees, thought they should investigate the need for legislation, and then suggest what form it should take.[58] When the Department produced a bill, it should be examined by the appropriate Committee before being submitted to the House of Commons. The Committee would subsequently take the Committee stage of the bill; they would also consider and report on any private Member's bill specially referred to it by either the Department or the House. He suggested elsewhere that a specialist

Committee should look after the Statute Book; that is, supervise the drafting and amending of bills, and prepare consolidation and codification bills.[59]

Point was given to these proposals by Lord Percy, who thought that Parliament's weakness in the field of legislation lay, not in a dearth of time or a waste of time, but in its lack of initiative in formulating bills. Committees should be able to do this.[60]

Should the Committee Control Expenditure?

Several writers have in mind that these Committees should exercise some sort of control over the spending of the Department. Lloyd George said they should be examining expenditure continuously,[61] and Dawkins thought that permanent specialist Committees should consider the Estimates in order to suggest economies (though without questioning the policies behind them).[62] Fellowes suggested more recently that a specialized Defence Committee should consider the Estimates of the relevant Departments and report to the house, by mid-May 1900, what economies (consistent with the Government policy underlying the Estimates) might be affected by them.[63]

But some suggestions go further, and say that the Committees should discuss the Department's proposed Estimates of expenditure before these are formally laid before the House. This pre-natal control, which may have been suggested by analogy with local government administration, is suggested, among others, by Pollard.[64] He also believes that the detailed discussion of the Estimates—at present done by the Committee of Supply and the Select Committee on Estimates—should be transferred to the Departmental Committees.[65]

Pollard envisaged a Finance Committee supervising the general arrangements. Laski, however, said that the Estimates were a reflection of Government policy, and that therefore it was wrong for the House to try to exercise 'pre-natal' control over them.[66]

Should the Committee Oversee a Department's Delegated Legislation?

Pollard is again among the several[67] who argue that all the statutory instruments which a Department makes should be subject to the approval of the appropriate Departmental Committee.[68] If the members of the Committee do not agree on the virtues of the proposed instrument, then it should require an affirmative resolution from the House of Commons before coming into force.[69]

The Particular Need for Certain Departmental Committees

Some of the demand for specialized Committees stems, not from a general principle, but from a belief that Parliament needs to be better informed of the workings of a particular Department. Thus from 1931—when a witness before a Select Committee averred that the Great War might conceivably have been avoided if there had been an active Foreign Affairs Committee which could have unearthed what was going on[70]—to 1957—when a motion was put down on the House of Commons Order Paper saying that Parliament lacked control over external affairs[71]—there have been proposals that the House should have a committee specializing in foreign affairs.

It has recently been suggested that there is an overwhelming case for more discussion of the affairs of British territories, some of which go unmentioned in the House for years at a time. The remedy proposed was a specialized Committee on Colonial Affairs.[72]

Another subject which suggests itself as suitable for non-party consideration inside a Committee room is Defence. Geoffrey de Freitas and Martin Lindsay have called for a Committee of this kind,[73] and have noted that Members of Parliament know less about the disposition of British forces than do the members of defence committees of foreign legislatures. Grimond included disarmament and the H-bomb as subjects on which Members needed more enlightenment.[74] Fellowes has pointed out that the creation of a Defence Committee would help to spread the debates on the Service Estimates over a longer period than at present.[75]

Laski suggested that there should be a series of Committees specializing in the nationalized industries.[76] He was writing before the creation of the Select Committee on Nationalized Industries, which has been set up sessionally since 1957, and which should, according to John Hall, be divided into two committees, covering the transport and power industries respectively.[77]

Pollard thought that, to make a start, a specialist committee of Members might be set up to concern itself with the Lord Chancellor's Department.[78]

We have noted above that it is sometimes suggested that Departmental Committees should concern themselves with the Estimates presented by those Departments, and that one suggestion was that there should be a supervisory Finance Committee. In step with this is Jennings' proposal that there should be a Committee concerning itself with the work of the Treasury.[79] This Committee would examine not only all the Estimates, but also the Finance Bill and the financial provisions of other bills; its essential functions would be informative, and it should not try to take the place of the Treasury itself. It could, however, act as a kind of court to which the Comptroller and Auditor General could appeal against the Treasury. This notion, apart from its legislative side, has affinities with the idea put by Campion to the Select Committee on Procedure in 1945: a Public Expenditure Committee should be set up, combining the dual roles of the present Estimates and Public Accounts Committee. This proposal was accepted and recommended by the Select Committee,[80] but it has never been put into effect, although it is still occasionally advocated.[81] Basil Chubb, however, after rehearsing the arguments for and against the proposal, concluded that it was not the entire answer.[82]

Relationship Between the Committee and the Minister

The matter of this relationship is clearly central to the whole problem, and most of the writers on the general subject touch on it. Their views, understandably enough, differ.

At one end of the spectrum are those who believe that the Minister should not only belong to the Committee, but be its Chairman. This was how Amery envisaged things,[83] as also did Cottenham,[84] and it is what the I.L.P. has consistently advocated.[85] Muir thought that, to avoid the Committee over-riding the Minister, he (or someone nominated by him) should be Chairman, with powers to exclude any question from consideration if it was a matter of policy.[86]

Greaves proposed that, if the Minister found that attendance at the Committee took too much time, he should delegate his duties to a junior Minister;[87] Jennings suggested that, normally, it should be the junior Minister's duty to attend.[88] The amendment moved by Leslie Hale to the Report of the Select Committee on Procedure in 1958/9 envisaged that at least one Minister should be a member of the proposed Colonial Committee, and that any Minister should be entitled to attend and speak, but not to vote.[89]

Others have thought that a meeting between Minister and Committee should only be occasional.[90] Laski (referring to a Foreign Affairs Committee) felt that it should have the power of summoning the Minister or his junior whenever it wanted.[91] Fellowes said it would probably be wiser if the Minister was not a member of the Committee, but such senior Ministers could be asked to attend occasionally.[92] This is approaching the other end of the spectrum, where Minister and Committee do not come together. Percy said that the Committee should agree to recommendations, which would then be passed on to the Minister.[93] The Committee, said Adams, should examine, discuss and advise; in the light of that, the Minister would decide.[94]

The Size and Constitution of 'Departmental' Committees

Most of the writers on the subject specify the need for 'small' or 'workmanlike' Committees; when an actual number is suggested, it is fifteen,[95] fifteen to twenty,[96] twenty-five,[97] or thirty-two to forty.[98] But two Members of Parliament, referring to a proposal to set up a Foreign Affairs Committee, thought that every Member should have a right to attend.[99]

All those who mention the topic agree that the political parties should be represented on these Committees in the same proportion as they are in the House.[100] It has also been suggested that the Committees should consist of Members of both Houses of Parliament.[101]

Incidental Powers, and Terms of Reference, of the Committees

A few writers think that these Committees should be 'unofficial' —that is, presumably, that they would act privately, have no specific warrant from their House, and make no Reports to the House.[102] As Salter puts it, their talks should have 'no legal effect'.[103]

But the majority look forward to official Committees, with specified duties and powers. Of these latter, it seems that all writers imply that the Committees will have the right—as enjoyed by most sessional Select Committees—to send for persons, papers, and records; this would enable them to examine witnesses from the Civil Service, and other appropriate experts. It is also implied that the Committees should have power to report their observations to the House—either annually, as Pollard and Muir suggested,[104] or when it suits them. It is sometimes said that these Reports should be the subject of debates on Supply days, which debates would in consequence be better-informed.[105]

Hale set out the duties of his proposed Colonial Committee with some care. The Committee would meet fortnightly, and could be convened specially if six of its members so desired. It would come to no decisions, except on various procedural points. Any subject could be added to its agenda on the requisition of a quarter of its members.[106]

Fellowes thought that his proposed Defence Committee's terms of reference should be to consider the Estimates of the relevant departments and report what economies, consistent with the policy implied in those Estimates, might be effected therein, and to consider such other matters as might be referred to it by the House or put before it by the Minister of Defence.[107]

Some little disagreement exists on the question of whether there should be a committee for each Department of State, or whether each Committee should concern itself with a 'subject area', which might take in the activities of several Departments. When explaining his plan for specialized Standing Committees, Dawkins suggested that there were four large subject areas: these were internal affairs and communications; social services; trade and industry; and Scottish affairs.[108] But the other writers on the subject seem to prefer the idea of considerably more; nine or ten, suggested Muir;[109] one for each Department, said, for example, Pollard[110] and Greaves.[111]

Conclusion

It can be seen that, over the years, there has been a widespread belief in the need for 'departmental' Committees of this kind.

Yet the opposition to the idea, allied of course to the formidable forces of inertia, has continued to prevail. It could be that this is due to the unwillingness of Members of Parliament to hand over any part of their powers to a Committee. Perhaps the then Speaker was right when, in 1931, speaking of the Estimates, he said: 'It cannot be suggested . . . that the rights of every Member to criticize them [should] be delegated to a small Committee upstairs.'[112]

So, if the system is to be introduced, it is probable that the relationship between the House and the Committees will have to be clearly and painstakingly worked out. A lot of thought has gone into the way the Committee's duties will be co-ordinated with those of the Minister; not so much into the way the House's rights over subordinate committees should be safeguarded. It might seem that the recent direct rejection by the House of a motion to set up a specialized Committee on Colonial Affairs (a Committee which was specifically designed as a prototype of other Committees) should have killed the hopes of those who believe in this idea.[113] But that division in the House took place along strict party lines, with the Government Whips on, and may have been less unambiguous than it seemed. It could be that, unnoticed, the House is in fact moving steadily nearer to an acceptance of the idea. Its recent creation of a Welsh Grand Committee, its continued support of a Select Committee on Nationalized Industries—these perhaps amount to something more significant than a formal counting of party strengths in the division lobbies.

(b) FINANCIAL PROCEDURE

The Criticisms

It can be argued that the House of Commons' most important function lies in its control of finance. Yet the working of this control is sometimes criticized, and indeed its very existence is occasionally called in doubt. Thus Samuel said that parliamentary control over finance had fallen into abeyance; that, once presented, every Estimate was approved as a matter of course.[114] Cottenham claimed that it was the Treasury, rather than Parliament, which decided the Estimates; Parliament voted what the Executive demanded: we were governed by officials.[115] These criticisms remain very current; in recent debates in the Commons, it has been said that the House has lost its former role of scrutinizer of the Estimates,[116] and that there is a need for much more control over public expenditure.[117] R. A. Butler, as Leader of the House, sums the matter up: 'I think we all feel . . . that there is something not quite right in the manner in which the House of Commons examines Supply.'[118]

The deterioration in the House's control over public expenditure has been a marked feature of post-war years. Lord Hinchingbrooke traced back to 1947 the procedure by which the House would agree to a Supply Vote formally—'on the nod'—in order to be able to stage in the time thus left over a general debate on Government policy.[119] But even before then, the 1946 Procedure Committee said that the examination of Estimates by the House had 'almost ceased to serve the purpose of financial scrutiny', and served merely as an excuse for debates on policy.[120] It is a fact, as R. A. Butler has pointed out, that the House really prefers a discussion of policy and politics to a detailed examination of Estimates.[121] There nevertheless exists a widespread feeling of discontent at the way huge sums of public money are voted with little or no debate. It is significant that the House's abdication of its duty to scrutinize details of expenditure has taken place in a period which has seen a vast increase in the size of State spending—especially on arms, welfare policies, and the nationalized industries. This has led to the paradoxical situation, noted by Grimond, that nowadays it is Members of Parliament who press for more expenditure, and the Executive who acts as the bulwark against further inflation and heavier taxation.[122]

Another, lesser, criticism is that the financial procedure of the House, in many of its aspects, is too complicated. The existence of two identical Committees of the Whole House—one of Supply, and the other of Ways and Means—was said by Jennings to introduce an element of 'mumbo-jumboism' into procedure.[123] Muir said that the way in which the national accounts were presented made it difficult for a Member to get 'any clear ideas as to the exact financial position of the nation'.[124] Peter Bromhead has described the Supply system as 'mysterious and esoteric'.[125] Hugh Dalton, writing on the Labour Party's proposals for reform in 1934, said that financial procedure took up too much time, and should be abbreviated.[126] Attlee, speaking in the House on the Army Estimates soon after, said it was unsatisfactory that they should have to discuss pages and pages of figures in a debate on the floor of the House.[127]

The Suggested Remedies

Attlee's suggested remedy was that Members should meet round a table, and have an official there to explain to them, by question and answer, the purpose behind each Estimate; a later speaker in the same debate answered that that was what the Public Accounts and Estimates Committees already existed to do.[128]

Many of the critics have called for an extension of the Committee system to cover what they feel to be a gap,[129] and there has been discussion of whether the existing Committees could not be made more effective.

The Select Committee of Procedure in 1931 advocated closer liaison between the Estimates and Public Accounts Committees, but this recommendation was later rejected by the Government of the day.[130] It was repeated, however, in 1944 when the National Expenditure Committee (which took the place of both Committees during the war) said that, in the light of their experience, there should be closer bonds between the Committees after the war than there had been before.[131] This in turn led to Campion's proposal to the 1945 Select Committee on Procedure, mentioned above, that both Committees should be coalesced into the one Public Expenditure Committee; the Procedure Committee recommended that this should be done, but the House has never authorized even an experiment along these lines. Chubb traced the arguments for and against this proposal, and himself believed that it was open to criticism.[132] It has, however, been aired again inside the House in recent years by Hinchingbrooke,[133] and outside by Paul Einzig, who visualized the new Committee operating through a number of specialist sub-committees.[134]

If part of the fault is in the fact that a Committee of the whole House is an unsuitable instrument for the examination of details, it can be argued that the House should create special Committees to do this kind of work on its behalf. Fellowes suggested to the

57

Procedure Committee in 1958 that the House should refer specific estimates to a Committee, and order the Committee to report on them by a certain time; the House would thereupon be able to vote the money in the assurance that the need for it had been examined.[135] This proposal was supported by, *inter alia*, Grimond,[136] but the Procedure Committee rejected it on a division.[137]

Another proposal by Hinchingbrooke was that every year ten Supply Days should be spent in an examination of the Estimates; a day or half a day should be allotted to a debate on the Estimates of each spending department.[138] Hinchingbrooke also lent his support to another suggestion put by Fellowes to the Procedure Committee. This was that the House—which normally votes a proportion of the Estimates 'on account' in March, and then actually grants the money in July—should, in July, only vote a further sum on account. The formal supply vote would then be made some time towards the end of the calendar year.[139] By interposing this extra step in Supply procedure, the House would ensure that finance was debated in the autumn—the time when, according to Birch (who was supporting the idea), decisions are taken about the Estimates for the following year.[140] But Fellowes' proposal had not been taken up by the Procedure Committee.

Other minds were turning to consider the work at present being done by the Select Committee on Estimates; its current terms of reference, said R. A. Butler,[141] left a gap, because it was not entitled to consider administrative policy. This point had been made a long while before, by the 1931 Select Committee on Procedure, which had recommended that the Select Committee on Estimates should no longer be debarred from considering matters of policy on which the Estimates were based. But this had been rejected by the Government, as it would have involved an encroachment on the powers of the Executive; however, it was said, where questions of administration and policy overlapped, with administration as the predominant factor, the Estimates Committee had hitherto considered it within its terms of reference to make recommendations, and the Government saw no objection to such an interpretation.[142] (Point was lent to this by a later Chairman of the Public Accounts Committee, who said that no power on earth could prevent a Committee going beyond its terms of reference, if it so wished.)[143] But it seems to be this bar on the discussion of pure 'policy' which makes some critics prefer the idea of setting-up new 'departmental' committees to keep an eye on expenditure, rather than to continue to use the Estimates Committee for this purpose.[144]

Another proposal of the 1931 Committee which has failed to be implemented is the suggestion that the Estimates Committee should have the help of a special technical staff. (Samuel suggested elsewhere the appointment of an expert officer, the 'Examiner of Estimates'.)[145] The Government thought this point could be met by having extra Treasury officials available to help the Committee; the National Expenditure Committee in 1941–42, envisaging a new Select Committee to review economies within the machinery of government, said that it would require an Assessor comparable in status with the Comptroller and Auditor General;[146] and a recent Committee has again recommended that the Estimates Committee should have the assistance of an accountant or specially qualified person.[147]

A leader in *The Times*[148] said that the three weaknesses of the Estimates Committee were its preclusion from studying policy matters, its lack of an independent watchdog such as the Comptroller and Auditor General, and the fact that the financial timetable turns each of its inquiries into a post-mortem. It advocated freedom from the restraint on discussing policy, and earlier reports from the Committee. The same newspaper said later that, as the departments now plan their estimates for something like two years ahead, parliamentary control would never mean much until the Estimates Committee could gauge the future financial consequences of policies on which the Government were embarking.[149]

Since the war, the Committee has had to consider whether it could not operate more efficiently if it had more effective powers of travelling to examine the expenditure of British public money abroad.[150]

It would clearly make the Estimates Committee a more formidable instrument if its Reports were, as a matter of course, debated by the House. A proposal that this should be done was made by Samuel in 1931,[151] and has been repeated in recent times by, amongst others, James MacColl[152] and Einzig[153]; R. A. Butler has come close to acquiescing to this on behalf of Government.[154] The 1946

Procedure Committee, in approving Campion's plans for a National Expenditure Committee, had also recommended that two Supply days should be spent each year in debating its Reports.[155]

Turning again to financial procedure in general, we note that Jennings elaborated his charge that this procedure was too complicated, and made suggestions for improving it. He felt it was unnecessary to have Votes on Account for each department; one single vote should be sufficient for all departments;[156] similarly, the separate Votes which have to be voted when the Supply guillotine falls should be divided on *en bloc*.[157] An annual Appropriation Bill was unnecessary; force of law should be given to the Estimates once they had been passed by the Committee of Supply; or, alternatively, the Appropriation Bill should undergo only one (i.e., a third) reading.[158]

Grimond has stressed the need for new machinery that would keep under review the provision of capital for the nationalized industries. His proposal was that an investment board should be set up for that purpose or, failing that, a Select Committee.[159] After a Government announcement that presaged a closer watch by the House over the spending of these industries, a leader in *The Times* pointed out the stagnation of management that might result. The idea that Parliament could itself run the industries was, it said, a delusion.[160]

Muir's suggestion was that the methods of presenting the Estimates and keeping the nation's accounts should be improved, so that they could be better understood.[161]

Various proposals have been voiced for accelerating the passing of the Finance Bill. Thus Ramsay MacDonald suggested, and Baldwin concurred, that it should be divided into two Bills—one dealing with taxation proper, which would be taken on the floor of the House, the other dealing with financial machinery which would be taken 'upstairs'.[162] It has been put forward that the Bills, or parts of the one Bill, could be taken at different times in the Session—administrative parts in the autumn, fiscal parts in the spring.[163] This idea of a divided Finance Bill was echoed by Jennings, who went further; the Taxation Bill would already have been discussed in Committee of Ways and Means, so all it would require would be a formal Third Reading.[164]

The Select Committee on Procedure in 1958/9 recommended that the Finance Bill should be committed, at least in part, to a Standing Committee each year; this, they said, was the greatest single economy that could be made in the time spent on the floor of the House.[165] A possible partition mentioned to them was that between the Bill itself, and the new clauses proposed to it.[166] It was suggested by one witness that the Standing Committee should be an especially large one,[167] and by another that the Committee should split up into two sub-committees, with the Financial Secretary and the Economic Secretary to the Treasury in charge respectively.[168] A Grand Committee has also been suggested.[169] But the proposal to discuss the Finance Bill in Standing Committee was seen by Einzig as further proof of Parliament's declining control over the nation's finances. The Committee stage, in Committee of the Whole House, is an occasion where the Government comes under the strongest pressure from public opinion. Because, under the Parliament Act, the Bill must be passed by early August, the Government is prepared to make concessions; by sending the Bill to Standing Committee, this inducement would no longer operate.[170]

The criticism, frequently heard in the thirties, about the lack of sufficient Supply days, and the disproportionate amount of time spent on Supplementary Estimates, seem largely to have been silenced by the changes introduced in financial procedure since 1945; though Fellowes, in his proposal to the Procedure Committee in 1958, thought that the House would be able to spend more time on Supply if some of its legislative duties were undertaken by Committees.[171] It was, however, to a more even spread of Supply days throughout the Session that the Procedure Committee turned its eyes.[172]

Grimond has suggested, as a remedy for irresponsible suggestions for increased expenditure, that no member should be allowed to advocate further expenditure without naming the tax which was to be increased to pay for it;[173] the need to stress that every proposed increase in the Estimates would be reflected in a rise in taxation has been mentioned by Birch.[174]

Financial Resolutions, which authorize the expenditure or taxation contained in Public Bills, are mentioned elsewhere.[175]

(c) LEGISLATION[176]

Although very many proposals have been made for improving Parliament as a legislative machine, very few envisage any radical alteration in the legislative process as such; the proposals, by and large, concern the individual stages of that process. Even Mosley and Cripps, who each looked forward to a much more widespread use of Orders in Council, envisaged that these would be made under General Acts which would have been passed by Parliament in the recognized way.[177] This is in line with what the Clerk of the House told the Procedure Committee in 1958; sooner or later, he said, Parliament would have to lay down general principles, and leave it to the Executive to administer them.[178] A change in the legislative system was, however, suggested by Sidebotham in 1930. He said that a bill's Committee stage in one House should be followed immediately by the same stage in the other House; on disputed points the Committees could sit jointly. Report stages in both Houses would then follow successively, as would Third Readings.[179]

But perhaps the proposal that goes furthest from the House's practice is that a bill which has not completed the legislative process by the end of a Session should be allowed to start the next Session at the point which it had reached before.[180] This had been urged by, for example, Lord Ponsonby in 1933,[181] and was repeated by Pollard in 1944.[182] Lloyd George is among those who have gone on record in opposition to this idea.[183]

Another far-reaching proposal, which was being widely canvassed in the 1930s, was that, as a matter of course, there should be a time-table regulating the progress of all bills. This would have the virtue of obviating tactics of obstruction, and Samuel, for instance, thought that a change along these lines was inevitable.[184] He felt that the Chairmen's Panel would be the right body to allocate what time should be spent on each stage. Sir Austen Chamberlain (repeating an original suggestion of his father) opined that an impartial Committee of Rules might be set up to do this; bills would not automatically be referred to the Committee for an allotment of time, but could be so referred if the member in charge of the bill required; the Committee could, if they thought fit, refuse to allow a time-table.[185] Dalton, writing in

1934, said the Labour Party proposed that a small Committee should be set up at the start of each Session, to allocate time on all Government bills and perhaps on other business.[186] Each Government bill would be given a detailed time-table; as in Samuel's and Chamberlain's proposals, the time-table would not itself be amendable or debatable in the House, but could be divided against. T. C. R. Moore, writing in 1935, said that every bill should proceed according to a time-table,[187] and this idea has been supported by Greaves.[188]

Guillotines for bills have, of course, been more frequently used since 1930, and have become almost respectable (though they remain always objectionable to the opponents of each bill). But no general ordinance, imposing guillotines on all or several bills, has been employed; and the time-table itself has always been open to debate and to amendment. There have been cases where the House has agreed to a voluntary time-table on important and contentious bills; 'It would', wrote Lord Campion, 'be a triumph for the spirit of conciliation if this procedure should come in future to be generally adopted.'[189]

Proposals for the automatic guillotining of the Committee stage of bills are mentioned later.

A proposal which could have important repercussions throughout the whole field of legislation was made by the Select Committee on Procedure in 1958/59. This was that an experienced officer or officers of the House should be appointed to assist private Members in drafting bills and amendments to bills.[190] Weight was given to this proposal by a Member who said, in debate, that it had cost him fifty pounds to prepare a bill; [191] but the idea was rejected on a division by the House.[192]

The Bill and its Initial Stages

In 1931, Captain (now Lord) Crookshank told the Select Committee on Procedure that he thought the introduction of all major political bills should be preceded by debates on general resolutions.[193] These general resolutions having been agreed to, a bill would be founded on them (in the same way as the Finance Bill proceeds annually). This might take up more of the House's time, but Second Reading debates could, in consequence, be shorter.

Jennings indeed thought that Second Reading itself might take place on resolutions rather than a bill.[194] After the resolution had been approved, the bill would be drafted.

Commander (now Sir) Stephen King-Hall suggested that, prior to legislation, the House should debate the Government's proposals as set out in a White Paper. This happens not infrequently now, but the proposal differs from current practice in advocating that, at the end of the debate, the House should vote on a number of Resolutions (which would be set out in the White Paper, and which would become the basis of the bill).[195]

A number of people have drawn attention to the importance of the Explanatory Memorandum which is sometimes attached to a public bill. Jennings thought there should be one to *every* bill, and hoped that it would give details not only of the proposals in the bill, but also the reasons for putting those particular proposals (instead of the possible alternatives) forward.[196] Pollard agreed that every bill should be accompanied by a memorandum, though this could, he added, be published separately.[197] Sidebotham believed that the reasons for a bill should be set out in the bill's preamble.[198]

It should be noted that the Select Committee on Delegated Legislation in 1953 decided against a proposal that every bill which proposed to delegate legislative powers should be accompanied by a special memorandum drawing attention to the fact. They thought the usual explanatory memorandum could cover this point, but made no special recommendation in the matter.[199]

Jennings drew attention to the blockage that might occur in the legislative machine at the drafting stage. He thought that the Parliamentary Counsel's services should be available to Private Members *after* their bills had been given a second reading (or, in his alternative suggestion, after the House had agreed to some resolutions on the subject—see above); a certificate from the Counsel would indicate whether or not any new principles had had to be introduced in the process of re-drafting.[200]

Muir, drawing attention to the unintelligibility of many statutes, suggested that a draftsman should re-draft every clause after a Committee had amended it.[201]

Hugh Dalton suggested that time could be saved by omitting all financial resolutions to bills: apart of course from the Ways and Means Resolutions on which the Finance Bill is founded.[202] Jennings elaborated the objections to these financial resolutions; debate on them largely repeated the Second Reading debate. He thought they could either be replaced by resolutions of the Standing Committee on Finance (which he elsewhere proposed), or be abandoned altogether.[203] Fellowes has put forward the view that the financial resolution should be considered, not as at present by a Committee of the Whole House, but by the Committee set up to consider the bill concerned.[204]

Committee Stage

It is towards the Committee stage of a bill that most proposals for legislative reform have been directed. Generally speaking, public bills go after Second Reading either to a Committee of the Whole House, or to a Standing Committee.

Occasional voices have been raised in favour of the principle that all bills should be considered on the floor of the House and not in Standing Committees. Baldwin thought that the right of all Members to take part in the detailed discussion of important measures should be safeguarded in this way;[205] more recently, Liberal Members of Parliament have proposed that bills should be automatically committed to a Committee of the Whole House rather than to a Standing Committee.[206] Ramsay MacDonald urged that there should be an automatic guillotine on the Committee stage of all bills taken on the floor of the House; this stage would thereby be more businesslike, and (presumably) more bills would be taken in that way.[207] This idea has recently been aired by Lord Hinchingbrooke, who, however suggested that bills of constitutional importance should be exempt.[208]

But much louder are the voices of those who believe that the Committee of the Whole House is the wrong instrument altogether for examining the details of bills. Thus Hollis wrote that it was a farce to send bills to a Committee when twenty-five or thirty members debated each proposal and 600 members were then required to vote on it;[209] and Jennings said that the Whole House was 'entirely incapable of dealing with Committee points'.[210]

The remedy they, and others, suggest is that the Committee stage of bills should be taken more often by Standing Committees.

Both Wheare[211] and Hollis[212] have drawn attention to the advantages of discussing details in the Committee atmosphere that is so lacking on the floor of the House. Some commentators however stress that certain bills—such as those of constitutional importance, and small uncontentious bills—should continue to go to a Committee of the Whole House;[213] the former because of the need to allow all Members the opportunity of taking part, the latter because they can be disposed of more quickly than in Standing Committee.[214]

Any scheme designed to make more use of Standing Committees must take note of the physical limitations of the House of Commons in this respect. Thus the Procedure Committee in 1958/59 heard of the difficulties of manning more committees, of staffing them, and of accommodating them.[215]

Schemes for the major reformation of the Standing Committee system have been put to Select Committees on Procedure in 1931, 1946, and 1958 by three Clerks of the House, Dawkins, Campion, and Fellowes.

Dawkins proposed that there should be five permanent Standing Committees, four of them responsible for a group of Departments, and one of them dealing solely with private members' bills.[216] The four groups would be Internal Affairs and Communications (which would include the Home Office, Transport, Agriculture, and the Post Office); Social Services (Ministries of Health, Education and Pensions); Trade and Industry (Ministry of Labour and Board of Trade); and Scottish matters. These Committees would consider all bills promoted by their Departments, and would consider their Estimates too.[217] The result would be the creation of Standing Committees of Members who had come to specialize in the subject, and this would result in better-informed debates.

Campion's proposals were more far-reaching, and took in a bill's Report—as well as Committee—stage.[218] He envisaged that, in addition to the Scottish Standing Committee, there should be two large Standing Committees consisting of seventy-five to a hundred members each. For the Committee stage of bills, each Standing Committee should consist of at least three sub-committees of twenty-five each, to whom fifteen should be added in respect of each bill. After the sub-committee had considered the bill, a drafting sub-sub-committee (of not more than seven members) would make drafting and consequential amendments. The bill would then be reported to the parent Standing Committee, which would consider it in the same way as the House does on Report stage. Thereafter, the House would not be able to amend the bill, but could recommit it to the Standing Committee if necessary. The bill, could, however, be debated on the motion for its consideration; once this was agreed to, the bill would stand for Third Reading. Any Member who had given notice of an amendment to a bill committed to a Standing Committee might, although not a member of that Committee, attend and move such amendment and take part in debate upon it, without, however, the right to vote.

Fellowes proposed that, after Second Reading, every public Bill should be sent either to the Committee on Unopposed Bills, a Committee on an opposed Public Bill, or the Committee on the Finance Bill. The Unopposed Bills Committee would consist of a Chairman and three Members; a Committee on an Opposed Public Bill would consist of a Chairman and fifteen Members; the Committee on the Finance Bill (which would consider other financial bills, in addition to the Finance Bill itself) would consist of a Chairman and thirty Members. If a bill was reported from a Committee without amendment, it would go at once for Third Reading; if it was amended, it would be recommitted to the former Committee for its Report stage. Fellowes repeated Campion's suggestion that Members should be allowed to speak in favour of their proposal even though they were not Members of the Committee; but the 1958/9 Procedure Committee rejected this proposal, saying that it might prove inconvenient to the Members concerned, as well as being a potential cause of confusion and of destruction.[219]

Some of the detailed points mentioned in these schemes have been spoken of elsewhere as desirable improvements in themselves. Thus Dawkins' idea of specialized Standing Committees has affinities with the whole scheme of Departmental Committees which is considered at length elsewhere.[220] Jennings took up Dawkins' proposal, but suggested there should be eight Committees.[221] Muir, too, thought Standing Committees should be composed of experts. An article in *Parliamentary Affairs* in 1958 pointed out that 80 per cent of time in Standing Committees was taken up by the 'added Members' (i.e. Members who used to be added to the Committee because of their particular interest in the bill), and suggested that the Committees could usefully be made up entirely of these experts.[222]

Hollis thought there was something to be said for allowing Standing Committees to co-opt experts from outside Parliament, perhaps with the power to speak but not to vote;[223] there was already so much consultation between the Government and outside interests about each bill's proposals, that the machinery should be made constitutional. Jennings believed that, instead of only giving advice to Ministers, the Civil Servants dealing with a bill should be open to questioning by the Committee, as should other experts.[224]

Suggestions are occasionally made that Standing Committees could profit from a change in their times of meeting. Since 1947, the only restriction on the times of sitting has been that the Committee could not meet between 1 p.m. and 3.30 p.m.; but the Committees have continued to meet, generally, on two or possibly three mornings in the week. The multiplication of sittings—combining morning and afternoon meetings—was criticized by Derek Walker-Smith as imposing an intolerable burden on Members.[225] Morning sittings are, generally, favoured by those who believe in 'full-time' Members of Parliament, such as Jennings,[226] and opposed by those who dislike that concept.

But if it is felt that Standing Committees take up too much of a Member's time, the remedy is at hand. In 1947 the House re-enacted a Standing Order[227] which had previously been repealed in 1933. This would allow the House to adjourn on certain days in order to facilitate the work of its Committees. But the Standing Order has never been used—neither in its new manifestation nor in its old.[228]

A proposal that would, its supporters say, make debates on a bill's details more purposeful, is that a time-limit should be imposed on the Committee stage of all bills; the Standing Committee would be ordered to report the bill by a certain date. This idea, which was suggested in an article in *Parliamentary Affairs* in 1958,[229] was said to give the Committee an incentive to make the best use of the time available; the actual time-table could be agreed either informally through the usual channels, or by some expeditious use of a resolution by the House. The Procedure Committee in 1958/59 favoured this idea, which they set out in some detail.[230]

However, certain opinions tend the other way—to the effect that no guillotines should be allowed to be imposed on a bill until there was definite evidence that obstruction was being met. This point had been made by Lord Winterton in 1931,[231] and was repeated by Captain Crookshank and Sir Charles MacAndrew in a debate in 1946;[232] it ran directly counter to Lloyd George's opinion which was that if a guillotine was to be imposed, it should be imposed from the outset and not after opposition had developed.[233]

For the Committee stage of uncontentious bills, Campion suggested that a Committee much smaller even than a Standing Committee should be employed.[234] Any bill, he said, to the Second Reading of which no Amendment had been moved might, on a motion by the Member in charge of it, be committed to the 'Uncontentious Bills Committee' of five members. After they had considered it, it would be reported back to the House, who would consider it in the same way as if it had come from a Standing Committee.

Lord Justice MacKinnon suggested that those parts of a bill which amounted to no more than the straightforward consolidation of existing enactments should, after Second Reading, be sent to the Joint Committee on Consolidation, etc., Bills.[235] This would, at the least, remove them from the field of controversy, and, at the most, diminish the opportunities for obstruction.

Later Stages

The proposals of Campion and Fellowes each, as we have seen, visualized that the Report stage of bills should be taken by a Committee rather than, as at present, on the floor of the House, and this idea won the distinguished support of Hugh Gaitskell.[236] The Procedure Committee, however, rejected this idea in 1959, saying that it was improper to depart from the principle that the Whole House should assume responsibility for the details of legislation.[237]

Several other writers, such as Greaves, have put forward the view that the Report stage, although taken on the floor, should be more restricted in time.[238] Similarly, Pollard thought that the Report stage and Third Reading of a bill could always be both dealt with in a single sitting in the House,[239] and Jennings felt that a rule to this effect should be incorporated in Standing Orders.[240] His view, which was attendant upon the change he had proposed for the Committee stage of bills, was that the Report stage would be considerably less important if the Committee had made a more thorough job of the amendments required. He suggested that amendments still necessary on Report should be moved to the Motion 'That the Bill as Reported be read a third time'; after they had been disposed of, the Motion, 'That the Bill as Reported (and amended) be read a third time' would be debated. This device would, he claimed, abolish the possibility of having a general debate on the operative clauses on Report, which would be repeated on the bill as a whole on Third Reading.[241]

Dawkins suggested that time could be saved if all drafting amendments at Report stage should be sent to a special committee of Members and legal experts;[242] Stewart echoed this idea.[243]

Percy was more forthright in his proposals. Apart from certain major bills, which would be debated in Committee and on Report on the floor of the House, all other bills, having passed through Standing Committee, should go straight to Third Reading.[244]

Jowett aimed to remove Report stage from the floor of the House; amendments put down for Report stage would be referred back to the Standing Committee to whom the bill itself would be recommitted, with instructions as to how to deal with them.[245] A point of detail recommended by the Select Committee on Procedure in 1958/9 was that all amendments imposing or varying a change which would be in order on Committee stage should in future be held to be in order on Report stage. This would obviate the need to recommit the Bill in order to consider such amendments.[246] But the House subsequently negatived this proposal.[247]

Private Bills

Private Bills are bills for the particular interest or benefit of some person or persons; as such they can be sharply distinguished from measures of public policy, and are treated by Parliament in an entirely different way. Unlike Public Bills, they are initiated, not by Members, but by parties outside the House; they are founded on Petitions made by those parties to Parliament, and opposed largely by other Petitions from other outside parties. In the Committee stage of the bill—which is its most important parliamentary hurdle—a small Committee of Members assesses the arguments for and against the bill, and either rejects it, or allows it to proceed (with any amendments they may think desirable). Other stages of the bill are generally formal, but it is always competent for either House to defeat a bill by direct action after a debate on the floor of the House.

Private Bill legislation has had a long and important history, but it is, says Campion, 'definitely on the downgrade'.[248]

Writing in 1930, Muir urged that the time taken by Private Bill legislative procedure in Parliament should be reduced by throwing more of the burden on to Government Departments.[249] This contention, like many of the other suggestions about Private Bill procedure made in the thirties, has been overtaken by events. The Provisional Order system which had, since the nineteenth century, been replacing the Private Bill system, was itself largely replaced in 1945 by the introduction of Special Procedure Orders;[250] and this new system is so young as to be without critics.

But if Private Bill legislation is on the downgrade, its vestigial rites have been attended by some hard words. It was in answer to powerful criticism of its procedure that a Joint Committee was set up in 1954. It reported in 1955,[251] and many of its proposals have duly been put into effect; since then, the critics have been quieter.

The above Committee, however, considered three proposals for the amelioration of Private Bill procedure which they did not recommend. These were: first, the adoption of a system of joint committees on Private Bills in substitution for the present procedure; secondly, the institution of a permanent Commission to authorize the extension to certain local authorities, or to local authorities generally, of powers granted to other 'pioneer' authorities; thirdly, the application to England and Wales of Scottish private legislation procedure.[252]

The Select Committee on Procedure recommended in 1959 that the presence of a motion on the Private Business order sheet should by itself be enough to block the progress of a private bill;

this would obviate the need for a Member to attend in person in order to obstruct the passage of the bill.[253]

(d) GENERAL PROCEDURAL REFORMS

Length of Sessions and Hours of Sitting

There has been a considerable change in the attitude of Members to these subjects. In 1931, Ramsay MacDonald said that the length of Sessions was 'absolutely intolerable'; Baldwin thought longer recesses were necessary to avoid the danger of government by tired men; and Winston Churchill said that a shorter session, of five to six months, would encourage the House to stick to the more important topics.[254] Gaitskell has said that the summer recess is too long, but that the Easter, and possibly the Christmas recess could reasonably be made longer.[255] Philip Goodhart, on the other hand, wanted to see the Christmas recess shortened.[256] But in all, nowadays, it is more usual for voices to be raised in simple protest against the length of the recesses (which are, in any case, shorter than in 1931).[257]

A suggestion with more life in it is that the House should revise its hours of sitting. Motions on the Order Paper in 1952, 1953 and 1956 all called for morning sittings of the House,[258] and several Members have referred to it in recent debates on Procedure[259] and in correspondence to The Times.[260]

Fellowes' scheme for procedural reform envisaged morning sittings on Mondays and Wednesdays; junior Ministers would be present to put the Government's point of view. Business to be taken would include debates to affirm or negate statutory instruments; opposed private business; Private Members' adjournment motions. There would be a time-limit on speeches, no divisions, and no counting out. The Select Committee which considered this scheme set out the case for and against morning sittings; on a division they rejected the idea,[261] and the House later confirmed this rejection.[262]

A fixed hour for the rising of the House has its supporters;[263] late sittings are frequently named as one of the principal causes of dissatisfaction with Parliament.[264] Fellowes has suggested that, if the House wishes to be able to sit late, the motion to enable it to do so should be debatable (at present, it must be decided without amendment and without debate).[265]

Another proposal has been that the parliamentary week should be shorter; this is sometimes allied with the suggestion (see under *Standing Committees*) that on one day a week the House should not sit, in order that its Committees could dispatch more business.

But all talk on the hours that the House should sit must really be reviewed in a broader context; for it is an aspect of two other wider problems. Should Parliament require full-time professional politicians? What ought to be the relationship between Parliament and the Executive? (For, even if Members gave up all other jobs in order to attend Parliament, Ministers would still have their Departments to attend.) These problems are discussed in Chapters IV and V of this book.

Speeches

The tool of the politician's trade is the speech. It is hardly surprising, then, that the writings considered in the present study are spattered with suggestions for improving the effectiveness of the speech as a weapon, or, at the least, of making sure that all Members have fair opportunities of employing it. Members constantly complain of the length of others' speeches; since 1930 there have been very many instances of this criticism and it is perhaps the aspect of procedure that gets more mention in the House than any other.

It is essentially a domestic problem and on the whole has had little attention from commentators outside the House; though Muir (who had, of course, himself been a Member for a short while in 1923–4) saw a point of principle involved. All Members should, he said, have the opportunity of expressing an opinion on each Government Bill; in those debates, then, some control of the length of speeches was essential.[266] But, by and large, it is within the House that the matter is generally raised. Frequently a major debate, in which few back-benchers have been able to speak, sparks off a new series of complaints. As a result, there has been a constant succession of demands for some sort of time-limit on speeches.

If members err, they do so in the face of constant exhortations from the Chair. Mr. Speaker Morrison, the late Lord Dunrossil, pointed out that the one attribute of a good speech within the reach of all is brevity.[267] Mr. Speaker Fitzroy said his experience was that short speeches were the most effective. Yet he had to admit that his previous advice on the subject had fallen on 'deaf ears or on unruly tongues'; Members, who promised to speak for ten minutes, went on for half an hour.[268]

Members have specified different time-limits as the desirable maximum. Thus a Whip suggested twenty minutes to the Select Committee on Procedure in 1931;[269] a self-denying ordinance by back-benchers, limiting themselves to fifteen minutes, was said in 1947 to have a good deal of support from both sides of the House.[270] Another suggestion has been that, during the dinner hour from seven o'clock to eight o'clock, there should be a ten-minute time-limit.[271] R. T. Paget has proposed the same limit should be in force between five o'clock and seven o'clock;[272] his suggestion led to a unanimous recommendation of the Select Committee on Procedure in 1958/9 that an hour should be set aside, at the discretion of the Chair, for five-minute speeches. They agree, however, that this could not be governed by Standing Order, but should be left to the good sense of Members.[273]

It has also been said that there is special need for a time-limit during debates under a guillotine. Campion (although he was on the whole opposed to a time-limit) thought that, if introduced, it could best begin in debates on Supplementary Estimates in Committee of Supply.[274] As noted above, Fellowes' scheme for morning sittings envisaged that speeches then would be limited in time.[275]

If a time-limit were introduced, allowance would need to be made for the time first taken up by interruptions, and then spent in answering them. The Speaker has pointed out that many speeches were prolonged for this reason;[276] and the recent Procedure Committee, in recommending short speeches, suggested that by convention Members should not be interrupted in them.[277]

Supporters of an imposed time-limit generally agree that front-bench speakers require special consideration, since they frequently have to make lengthy expositions of, for example, a bill.[278] On the other hand, it is precisely these lengthy speeches that some back-benchers object to and think should be curtailed.[279]

Various references have been made in the House to a voluntary time-limit operating in some Scottish debates. Thus in a 1936 debate on the Scottish Estimates, speeches were limited to fifteen minutes.[280] Other references, in 1941, 1948 and 1953 indicated that some degree of restraint continued to be shown by Scottish Members.[281]

It is rare that a case is made out in favour of the *status quo*; when it is, it is based on the sanctity of preserving minorities' rights, and on the dissatisfaction which a formal time-limit would cause.[282] Thus, one Member described a debate of short speeches as a parliamentary Children's Hour.[283] It has also been said that the thing Ministers fear most is the long, well-informed speech of criticism.[284] The Government, when questioned for their views on the subject, have always said that it is a matter that must be left to the good sense of individual Members;[285] a voluntary time-limit might be worth trying.[286] When appeal is made to the Speaker, his invariable reply is that he has no powers in the matter —the remedy must lie with the House.[287]

Until the 1958/9 Procedure Committee, the nearest the House had got to considering it had been in the deliberations of the Select Committee on Procedure in 1946. They heard no evidence in favour of the idea, and they did not recommend it.[288] It may be that their final opinion mirrored that of the Member who claimed in 1948 that the main trouble was not excessive oratory, but an overloaded parliamentary programme.[289] It could be that they were aware of the paradox pointed out elsewhere—that some speeches, which were very short in time, seemed very long to the House.[290]

Herbert Morrison has drawn attention to the deleterious effect of Members making speeches which do not try to follow what has been said before; as a result, there is no cut and thrust.[291] 'What kills debate', said Grimond, is 'the old rule that it is Buggins's turn now, and if Buggins wants to talk about something different from what went before, he gets up and does so.'[292] Speeches such as these, said Charles Pannell, should be ruled out of order.[293]

As a means by which more Members can have their opinions made public, Kennedy suggested in 1936 that Members should be allowed to circulate in the Official Report those speeches which they had not been able to make orally in the Chamber.[294] This suggestion has recently been taken up by Anthony Wedgwood Benn,[295] but the Procedure Committee of 1958/9 found the practice undesirable.[296]

If some Members have favoured written speeches, there has been no encouragement for speeches which are read out in the House. Opinions on this point are frequently expressed; specific objection was taken in 1947 to the delivery of prepared winding-up speeches, which made no answer to the detailed points raised during the debate.[297] But, as the Speaker pointed out in 1952, although the conventions of the House still stood out against the reading of speeches, it had 'become the practice in recent years for Ministers to be allowed greater latitude in this respect'.[298]

In view of Members' sensitivity on the matter of their speeches, it is not surprising that the Speaker has often found his duty of choosing Members to speak an invidious one. Thus it is sometimes objected that, in his zeal to see that all points of view are heard, he is too indulgent towards minority parties; and the Government back-benchers get less than their fair share of the House's time.[299] It has also been suggested that his eye should rest less frequently on the more garrulous of Members,[300] though this was a proposal that he had already scouted.[301]

A Member suggested that there should be a rationing of time among Members, to make up for the uncertainty of the favours of the Speaker's eye: he could have got little comfort from the then Father of the House, whose experience was that the people who didn't get called often were, in general, the people no one wanted to hear.[302]

Other suggestions have been that speakers should be chosen by ballot; that those who write to the Speaker, asking to be called, should automatically be disqualified; and that those who wish to speak, but on whom the Speaker's eye is not going to alight during a particular debate, should be informed, so that they no longer need wait in hopeless expectation. It has been said that a list should be circulated beforehand of those Members who are likely to be called on to speak in a debate, as happens in the House of Lords.[303] Criticism was also made of the conversations which took place behind the Speaker's chair and which appeared to influence the choice of who should speak in the debate.[304]

The Speaker's answer to these criticisms has been that he had to see that every expression of opinion had a fair chance, and that he tried to call all minorities; he chose speakers from amongst those who continually rose just as much as from those who wrote to him.[305] On another occasion, a Speaker had said that it had always been the practice for minorities to get more than a generous share of time, and that to call on speakers according to the numerical strengths of parties would not improve the character of debates.[306]

It is a fact that a Member, anxious to be able to put his point of view, and the Speaker, charged with the duty of preserving the House's traditions, must sometimes be at odds. This is most clearly seen in the objection that Members take to the 'right' of Privy Councillors to be heard whenever they offer themselves to speak, and it has been in the post-war period that this right has been most heavily attacked. Constant objection has been taken to it; a number of Motions on the Order Paper have called for its rescission.[307] But when the subject is raised in the House, the Speaker can do no other than point out that the traditions and practice of the House have always allowed Privy Councillors a greater right to be called.[308]

However, when the Select Committee on Procedure came to consider the matter in 1958/9, they reported that the rule no longer operated in the best interests of the House; they suggested that Privy Councillors should have only the same rights as other Members in asking supplementary questions, and, in debate, the Speaker should not be bound to call them in preference to other members. This virtual abolition of the rule was, they thought, better than the modifications of it which had been suggested to them—namely, that Privy Councillors should only have priority when the debate was on a subject for which they had previously been departmentally responsible, or that two (or more) Privy Councillors should not be called in succession.[309] The House, however, negatived the recommendation of the Select Committee.[310]

Question Hour

The right to ask a Minister for a public reply to a particular Question is amongst the most prized of a private Member's privileges.[311] The popularity of the Question has grown, and in 1931 the Procedure Committee was told by the Clerk of the House that it might become necessary to reduce the number that a Member is allowed to ask orally, from three to two per day.[312] This idea, though supported by MacDonald and Sinclair,[313] did not commend itself to the Committee; but another Select Committee (which had been set up to consider the relationship between Parliament and the nationalized industries) recommended the change twenty years later,[314] and it has since been adopted. Kennedy, in 1931, was more drastic; he suggested that Members should only be allowed to ask one oral Question per day.[315] Cyril Osborne, in 1959, suggested that a Member should only be allowed to put down one Question to a particular Minister on a particular day.[316]

An alternative that Dawkins put to the Committee was that the Speaker should be allowed (possibly with the Member's consent) to direct that a Question should be 'unstarred'. This proposal was supported by Sir Austen Chamberlain,[317] but the Committee did not recommend it.

But the Committee did propose that a new class of Questions—'daggered' Questions—should be introduced;[318] these should be for accelerated written answer. The House did not give effect to this proposal, which has, however, been recently resuscitated by Wedgwood Benn.[319]

A different suggestion, put forward by de Freitas, was that the total number of Questions which a Minister should be required to answer on a particular day should be limited.[320] (At present, the whole of Question Hour can be taken up by Questions to one Minister.) The 1958/9 Procedure Committee turned down a suggestion along these lines.[321]

In order to prevent a Question becoming 'stale', the same Procedure Committee recommended that not more than three weeks' notice should be allowed of a Question.[322]

The idea is sometimes voiced that more time should be allowed for Questions. It has been suggested that there should be a Question Hour on Fridays; but the Leader of the House thought that this was not a day that saw the House at its brightest.[323] With the House's decision in 1958, that Member's letters to Ministers were not privileged, a number of Members thought that Question Hour should be extended to ninety minutes in order to give more time for the (privileged) laying of grievances before Ministers by means of Questions.[324] A 'modest proposal' by Tom Driberg has been that Question Hour should at least last a full hour.[325]

The 1931 Procedure Committee did not accept the Clerk's suggestion[326] that they could usefully review the rules which have accreted on the subject of Questions, and these have continued to grow up piecemeal. They considered, but did not concur in, the proposal that the right to ask a supplementary Question should be limited to the asker of the substantive Question.[327]

Wedgwood Benn has recently suggested that no Minister should be allowed to refuse an answer to an oral Question, except with the consent of the Speaker.[328] Emrys Hughes thought, in 1949, that Members should be allowed to put parliamentary Questions to the Leader of the Opposition, in addition to Ministers.[329] It has been suggested by a Procedure Committee that the Prime Minister's Questions should be taken at a fixed hour—3.15 p.m.[330]

In Fellowes' scheme for procedural reform, he suggested that Questions should be taken, not in the House, but in three Grand Committees, which would sit, twice a week, at an hour when the House was not sitting.[331]

The most radical change that has been suggested, however, is that by Lord Percy. Question Hour should, he thought, be abolished, and its time taken up by short debates on topical matters.[332] Sidebotham was thinking along the same lines; better five or ten Questions exhaustively treated, than one hundred answered perfunctorily. These five or ten should be chosen by a small committee of members, and the rest should be answered in writing.[333]

Summing up their opinions on Question Hour, the 1945 Procedure Committee said it was 'perhaps the readiest and most effective method of parliamentary control over the action of the executive'. Therefore the very powerfulness of the right imposed a proportionate responsibility on members in its' use; Questions should only be put down when other and less formal methods have failed to produce a satisfactory result, or when some information or action is urgently desired.[334]

The 1958/9 Procedure Committee said that the root of the problem of Question Hour lay in the fact that supplementary questions were more frequent and longer, and the answers longer, than they used to be. They urged the House to support the Speaker when he tried to curtail questions.[335] This view has been echoed by *The Times*, which expressed the hope—'a naïve hope'—that members would exercise more discrimination in their questioning.[336]

Divisions

Among the more bizarre discoveries of this research has been the fact that H. G. Wells, while spanning *The Work, Wealth and Happiness of Mankind*, [337] should have paused to observe that the method of voting in the House of Commons—in contrast to that used in Texas—was 'processional' and inefficient. Yet, if it may not have such worldwide implications, voting procedure in the Commons is certainly a matter that frequently engages the mind of those who think about Parliament. Ross lists it first among the causes of dissatisfaction with Parliament today;[338] and it was repeatedly adverted to in a recent correspondence in *The Times*.[339] Moreover, every Procedure debate in the House of Commons brings out complaints on the system employed.

The usual epithet used—'time-wasting'—is hard to gainsay; in 1946, the average time taken for a Division was 10·8 minutes, and it sometimes requires two or more Divisions to conclude the debate on a question.[340] Yet experienced parliamentarians do not always agree that the system is bad. Baldwin thought it was useful to relieve tension: 'In the heat generated by the gag ... a walk through the lobbies restored the House to a sense of perspective.'[341] Herbert Morrison said that, 'Anyway, moving through the Division Lobbies is a useful and pleasant social occasion.'[342] An Opposition Chief Whip found in the system 'something rather wonderful'.[343]

The critics of the present system have suggested a number of palliatives. First, that a mechanical, press-button system of voting could be introduced. Secondly, that various improvements could be made in the present arrangements. Thirdly, that Members should be allowed to vote, *in absentia*, by proxy. Fourthly, that all Divisions should take place at a convenient, pre-arranged, time. Fifthly, that there should be fewer Divisions.

(i) Mechanical Voting: This is frequently put forward by

commentators inside and outside Parliament; both Pollard and Greaves suggest it. It is rare, however, that the scheme is set out in detail, so that the practical difficulties are hard to assess. One critic of the idea, thinking it required specified seats in the Chamber for each Member, believed that a larger House would have to be built before the scheme could be introduced.

One practical scheme was put before the Select Committee on Procedure in 1946.[344] By it, Division time could be cut down, but it would still require seven and a quarter minutes; for the great proportion of the time taken is the six minutes which must be allowed for Members to get to the Chamber from wherever they are. There were various shortcomings in the device, and the Committee felt it was 'neither so convenient nor so accurate a means of counting votes and recording names as the present method'.

Another scheme was considered by the Select Committee on Procedure in 1958/9; this was calculated to cut the time of a division down to six minutes. In dismissing the scheme, the Committee could only cite the congestion which they deemed to be inevitable in the lobbies as a result, and the loss of the present amenities in the lobbies.[345]

(ii) It has been suggested that the division would take less time if there were six division clerks, or eight tellers; or if the present division lobbies could be duplicated somewhere else in the House.[346]

(iii) Proxy voting has been advocated, amongst others, by a leader in the *Manchester Guardian*, as a minor reform that would help;[347] and it has been advocated within the House.[348] Hollis has drawn attention to the Norwegian example, where each Member has a substitute who can perform the Member's duties when he is away;[349] and Acland has also stressed the desirability of substitutes.[350]

The 1958/9 Procedure Committee turned down the idea of proxies, including those for sick Members. They did not take up two other ideas—that Members should be allowed a proxy vote once a month,[351] or that they should be allowed a registered pair twice a month.[352]

(iv) If it was known at what time Divisions were going to take place, Members could arrange other engagements without the fear that in so doing they might miss an important vote; thus they sometimes suggest that the procedure be changed in this regard.[353] Also, the vote on 'prayers' which may not end till late at night, should be held over until the next day.[354]

The idea is never fully worked out. Sir Herbert Williams cited the absurdity of holding the Divisions that would follow a Committee stage, all together, at a time when people have forgotten the detailed points that were at issue.[355]

(v) When Members suggest that there should be fewer Divisions,[356] they appear to do so out of pious hope rather than practical expectation; Parliament works by means of debates leading up to Divisions, and it is hard to say how its right to divide can be restricted. Ramsay MacDonald, however, suggested in 1931 that it was unnecessary to hold Divisions on the Closure, since these were a foregone conclusion;[357] and the 1945/6 Procedure Committee was reminded that the Speaker already had power to require a vote to be taken by counting Members, for and against, in the House, after only two minutes, if he thought the division had been unnecessarily claimed. The Committee did not however, as urged, recommend a more frequent use of this Standing Order.[358]

Procedural Miscellanea

There are, of course, innumerable proposals made from time to time for improving the minutiae of parliamentary procedure. These hardly rate attention in a project of this kind but, taken together, they might conceivably amount to a 'reform of procedure'; some of the more interesting suggestions, most of them made in recent debates on Procedure, are accordingly listed here.

Adjournment Motions. The half-hour debates at the end of each day's sitting, in which some private Members can raise matters on their own initiative, should be moved to an earlier part of the sitting.[359]

Goodhart has also expressed the wish that these debates should be longer and more frequent.[360]

As noted above, Fellowes suggested that these debates should take place in the morning. MacAndrew put forward the idea that no adjournment motion should be allowed after 11.30 p.m. Other suggestions have been that incidental references to legislation should be allowed in them, and that any change of subject should be announced beforehand.[361]

Black Rod, who summons the Commons to attend in the Lords to witness the Royal Assent to bills, should not do so in the middle of a debate.[362] His entry should be at fixed, pre-ordained times.[363]

The Business of the House should be known longer in advance.[364]

The Closure, which at present requires a hundred assenting votes, should only require a simple majority of the House in its favour.[365] The Procedure Committee in 1958/9 saw no reason for lowering the number required for the closure (and for the quorum), as had been suggested to them by the Government Chief Whip.[366]

A Count, which took place two minutes after it had been called for, should allow more time for Members to get to the Chamber.[367]

Debates on large general topics should be split up into more manageable compartments.[368] Furthermore, it is said that the House could not lead public opinion on contemporary problems if it went on fixing its debates ten days ahead.[369]

A 'Judge' for the House of Commons should be appointed. He would be a non-party officer of the House, who would assess impartially the cases put by each side during a debate.[370]

Ministerial Statements are at present made after Question Hour. Since they are made, as it were, *in vacuo*, and not on a formal motion, debate on them is irregular; the disorderly kind of debate that follows them was described by Kenneth Pickthorn as one of the worst abuses of procedure.[371] It has been suggested that Ministers should move the adjournment if they wish to make a statement.[372]

The Order Paper should be made more readily intelligible.[373]

Pairs, it is so said, should be easier for Members to arrange.[374] The Procedure Committee in 1958/9 declared themselves satisfied with the present arrangements, and did not take up the idea of the pre-war 'pairing book' that was favourably mentioned to them.[375] The whole system of pairing, however, has never been officially recognized by the House. It remains a strictly private enterprise.

Public Petitions were once a powerful means of bringing pressure to bear on the House. The procedure on them should be changed, to make them more effective today.[376]

Points of Order are made promiscuously, and should be penalized.[377] One Member counted forty-two false points of order in a month.[378]

A Procedural Committee should be set up automatically at the start of each session, and should make reports from time to time to the House.[379]

Standing Orders should be more amenable to change; at present, they were narrowed down from precedent to precedent. There should be a sessional Select Committee which would consider the working of an Order whenever a hundred Members asked for it to be amended.[380]

Standing Order No. 9 (Adjournment on a definite matter of urgent public importance) was falling into desuetude and should be more liberally interpreted.[381] Fellowes, who thought these debates could best take place at the end of the day's sitting, urged that the onus of defining 'urgency' and 'public importance' should be placed on the House; the Procedure Committee went some of the way with him, and recommended a rather wider interpretation of the Order.[382] The House, however, did not lay down any changes in the procedure, on the understanding that discussions would take place to see if any relaxation could be afforded.[383]

The Swearing-in of Members at the start of a new Parliament took an inordinate time, and should be curtailed.[384] (Jennings suggested this might be done before a justice of the peace, or before the Speaker privately.[385])

Conclusion

We have seen that, amongst the suggestions for reform of Procedure, it is the proposed system of Departmental Committees that offers change on the broadest front—spanning as it does Parliament's three functions, financial, legislative and deliberative. Furthermore, in the piecemeal criticisms of to-day's Procedure, it is the Committee stage of bills, and the Commons' control of finance by means of its Committees, which come in for the most comment. It becomes clear that the core of any large-scale procedural reform lies in the use the House of Commons makes of its Committees.

There is visible, too, a trend towards smaller Committees—from a Committee of the Whole House to a Standing Committee, from a Standing Committee to a Committee of the size of to-day's Select Committees. Underlying all this, perhaps, is the shining way in which Select Committees have in the past been able to deal with controversial matters in a non-party way.

But, before any proposal is advocated to increase greatly the work done by Commons Committees, three notes of warning should be sounded. In the first place, the House has always insisted on the *subordinate* character of its Committees; they are never allowed executive powers; and the House reserves its right to reject, or even ignore, any suggestions they make. So any change which will increase the effectiveness of Committees should allow for the House's traditional concern to remain the master of all that happens in its subordinate bodies.

Secondly, if too many important decisions are to be taken by small groups of members, one may be getting away from the principle that each elected representative ought to have an equal opportunity of influencing events.

Thirdly, the success of Select Committees in the past may have been due in part to a careful selection of matters which have been referred to them. If they had to deal with too many subjects of party-political controversy, it could be that they would not prove so successful. There is the danger that, if you move too many subjects from the floor of the House to the Committee rooms, the party-political guns will be moved with them.

The chances are that if a change is made in the way the House uses its committees, then the change will come gradually. It is possible that alterations will come more rapidly to the way the House controls finance. Because Government expenditure has increased so vastly, it has become the more difficult to control in detail; the House's dilemma is that, because of such a great increase, control is all the more essential. Einzig has stressed the importance of the House recovering the spirit which formerly inspired it in favour of retrenchment;[386] it seems that a change of spirit is essential, and, slowly, the House seems to be becoming aware of the fact.

But, if the House proves unwilling to make any basic and major change in the way it approaches its work, there are clearly very many minor ways in which it could improve its procedure. Morning sittings, mechanical voting, some form of limitation in length of speeches—reforms such as these could not but make the House a more bearable and perhaps more efficient assembly.

NOTES AND REFERENCES*

[1] H.C. Deb. 617, c. 70.
[2] *ibid.* c. 38.
[3] See articles by A. H. Hanson in *Parliamentary Affairs*, Vol. X, No. 4, and Vol. XI, No. 1.
[4] This important aspect of the relationship between Parliament and the Executive is considered in the present chapter because of its essentially 'procedural' nature. Other problems and proposals for reform are discussed in Chapter V.
[5] H.L. Deb. 86, cs. 791ff.
[6] H.C. 161 of 1931, Q. 656.
[7] Greaves: *The British Constitution*, 1948, p. 50.
[8] *English Review*, Vol. LIX, 1934, pp. 29–39, 163–74.
[9] *Public Administration*, Vol. XXIV, 1946, pp. 75–85.
[10] Lord Campion and others, p. 281.
[11] H.C. 161 of 1930/1, Q. 408.
[12] Greaves, pp. 49–51.
[13] Amery, pp. 53–4.
[14] Lord Campion and others, p. 34.
[15] *ibid.* p. 84.
[16] Spectator, 10th November 1933, pp. 653–4.
[17] *English Review*, Vol. LIX, 1934.
[18] H.C. 161 of 1930/1, Q. 481.
[19] Lord Campion and others, p. 34.
[20] *Manchester Guardian*, 22nd July 1957, p. 6.
[21] H.C. 92 of 1958/9, pp. xlix–l.
[22] Lord Campion and others, p. 34.
[23] Grimond: *Manchester Guardian, loc. cit.*
[24] Fitzroy: H.C. 161 of 1930/1, p. 406.
[25] Lord Campion and others, p. 83.
[26] Lord Cottenham: *English Review*, Vol. LIX, 1934; and John Hall: H.C. Deb. 617, c. 113.
[27] Adams: *Listener*, Vol. VII, 17th February 1932, pp. 236–7.
[28] Grimond: *Manchester Guardian, loc. cit.*
[29] Lord Campion and others, p. 119
[30] Jennings, p. 141.
[31] Lord Campion and others, p. 83.
[32] *ibid.* p. 33.
[33] See *Speed up Law Reform*, Fabian Research Series, No. 194, 1958, p. 25.
[34] A better and more recent example might be the Select Committee on Nationalized Industries.

* All references to Jennings in this chapter are to his *Parliamentary Reform*.

[35] *Listener, loc. cit.*
[36] H.C. 92 of 1958/9, Q. 276.
[37] *ibid.* p. 18.
[38] *ibid.* para. 47.
[39] *Manchester Guardian*, 13th November 1952.
[40] H.C. 161 of 1930/1, p. 154. Jowett's views were mostly expressed before the period covered by this research, but his name should be remembered as one of the chief begetters of the specialized committee system.
[41] Jennings, pp. 126–9.
[42] H.C. 161 of 1930/1, p. 259.
[43] Laski, pp. 87–8.
[44] Lord Campion, and others pp. 33–4.
[45] H.C. 92 of 1958/9, p. xxv; also p. xlix.
[46] Writing on behalf of Mosley's New Party: *Political Quarterly*, Vol. II, 1931.
[47] H.C. 92 of 1958/9, Q. 1161.
[48] H.C. 161 of 1930/1, p. 406.
[49] *Political Quarterly*, Vol. II, 1931.
[50] *Manchester Guardian*, 25th May 1934.
[51] Morrison, pp. 155–9.
[52] At present, bills are sent after second reading to a committee—either a Committee of the Whole House, or a Standing Committee (which consists of from twenty to fifty members). These Committees do not specialize in a particular class of bill, although the Scottish Standing Committee deals with bills of all kinds that pertain to Scotland. The Scottish Grand Committee—consisting of all Scottish members, plus ten others—holds general debates on Scottish matters, some of them being virtually Second Reading debates on Scottish bills, and considers the Scottish Estimates; the Welsh Grand Committee, consisting of all Members for Welsh constituencies, and twenty-five others, holds general debates on Welsh matters. None of these Committees, of course, initiates legislation.
[53] Jennings, p. 145.
[54] H.C. 161 of 1930/1, p. 154.
[55] H.C. 92 of 1958/9, p. 18.
[56] *Manchester Guardian*, 13th November 1952.
[57] *Political Quarterly*, Vol. IV, 1933.
[58] *Speed up Law Reform*, pp. 24ff.
[59] *How to Reform Parliament*, 1944, p. 43.
[60] *Spectator*, 10th November 1933.
[61] H.C. 161 of 1930/1, pp. 41–60, *passim.*
[62] *ibid.* Appendix 6.
[63] H.C. 92 of 1958/9, p. 18.
[64] *Speed up Law Reform*, pp. 24–5.
[65] *How to Reform Parliament*, pp. 43–4.
[66] Laski, p. 37.
[67] Others include Cripps, Muir, Wise and Lord Eustace Percy.
[68] *How to Reform Parliament*, p. 43.
[69] *Speed up Law Reform*, pp. 24–5.
[70] H.C. 161 of 1930/1, Q. 3111.
[71] Motion, 22nd January 1957.
[72] H.C. 92 of 1958/9, p. 1.
[73] H.C. Deb. 581, c. 697; and the *Observer*, 14th December 1958.

[74] *Manchester Guardian*, 22nd July 1957.
[75] H.C. 92 of 1958/9, p. 18.
[76] Laski, p. 91.
[77] H.C. Deb. 617, c. 113.
[78] *Speed up Law Reform*, p. 25.
[79] Jennings, pp. 127–9.
[80] H.C. 189 of 1945/6.
[81] e.g. H.C. Deb. 557, c. 1322.
[82] Chubb: *The Control of Public Expenditure*, 1952, p. 239.
[83] Amery, p. 53.
[84] *English Review*, Vol. LIX, 1934.
[85] H.C. 161 of 1930/1, Q. 1775; and Memo (unpublished) to Select Committee on Procedure in 1945.
[86] H.C. 161 of 1930/1, p. 259.
[87] Greaves, pp. 42–4.
[88] Jennings, p. 144.
[89] H.C. 92 of 1958/9, p. 6.
[90] Thus Molson (unpublished memo to Select Committee, 1945); and H.C. Deb. 400, c. 1093.
[91] Laski, pp. 87–8.
[92] H.C. 92 of 1958/9, Q. 274–7.
[93] *Spectator*, 10th November 1933.
[94] *Listener*, 17th February 1932, pp. 236–7.
[95] Lloyd George, Pollard.
[96] Fellowes (Defence Committee).
[97] Greaves.
[98] Hale (Colonial Committee).
[99] Amendment to Motion, 22nd January 1957.
[100] Jennings, Pollard, Greaves, Brogan, etc.
[101] e.g. by Amery, p.53.
[102] e.g. Young, Salter and Wheare.
[103] Lord Campion and others, pp. 118–9.
[104] *Speed up Law Reform*, pp. 24–5; and H.C. 161 of 1930/1, p. 259.
[105] e.g. Lloyd George, H.C. 161 of 1930/1, Q. 391.
[106] H.C. 92 of 1958/9, p. 16.
[107] *ibid.* p. 18.
[108] H.C. 161 of 1930/1, Appendix 6.
[109] H.C. 161 of 1930/1, p. 259.
[110] *How to Reform Parliament*, p. 43.
[111] Greaves, pp. 49–51.
[112] H.C. 161 of 1930/1, p. 406.
[113] H.C. Deb. 617, c. 171–4.
[114] *Political Quarterly*, Vol. II, 1931.
[115] *English Review*, Vol. LIX, 1934.
[116] e.g. Ellis Smith, H.C. Deb. 557, c. 1313.
[117] Lord Boothby, H.C. Deb. 581, c. 688; see also H.C. Deb. 619, cs. 1315–75 *passim*.
[118] H.C. Deb. c. 1368. 16th March 1960.
[119] H.C. Deb. 16th March 1960, c. 1317.
[120] 3rd Report of Select Committee on Procedure, 1946, para. 36.
[121] H.C. Deb. 16th March 1960, c. 1373.
[122] *Manchester Guardian*, 22nd July 1957.

[123] Jennings, p. 119.
[124] Muir, p. 224.
[125] *Parliamentary Affairs*, Vol. XII, Nos. 3 & 4, pp. 337–48.
[126] *Political Quarterly*, Vol. V, pp. 469–79.
[127] H.C. Deb. 262, c. 1668–9.
[128] H.C. Deb. 262, c. 1764.
[129] The proposals to set up 'Departmental' Committees, which might concern themselves, *inter alia*, with a department's expenditure, are considered above.
[130] H.C. Deb. 277, c. 669–70.
[131] H.C. 122 of 1943/4.
[132] Chubb, *The Control of Public Expenditure*, 1952, p. 239.
[133] H.C. Deb. 619, c. 1321–2.
[134] Einzig: *The Control of the Purse*, 1959, p. 330.
[135] H.C. 92 of 1958/9, Q. 191, 184, 284.
[136] *ibid*. p. 122.
[137] *ibid*. p. 48.
[138] H.C. Deb. 619, c. 1323.
[139] H.C. 92 of 1958/9, p. 13.
[140] H.C. Deb. cs. 1341–2, 16th March 1960.
[141] H.C. Deb. cs.1371–3, 16th March 1960.
[142] H.C. Deb. 277, cs. 669–70.
[143] H.C. 189 of 1945–6, Q. 4091.
[144] e.g. H.C. Deb. c. 1345, 16th March 1960.
[145] *Political Quarterly*, Vol. II, 1931.
[146] H.C. 120 of 1941/2, p. 38.
[147] H.C. 184 of 1953/4, para. 39.
[148] *The Times*, 18th March 1960.
[149] *ibid*. 27th July 1960.
[150] See, for example, H.C. 149 of 1953/4; and H.C. 290 of 1953/4.
[151] H.C. 161 of 1930/1, Q. 2537.
[152] H.C. Deb. 510, c. 615–6.
[153] Einzig, p. 330.
[154] H.C. Deb. 16th March 1960, c. 1373.
[155] H.C. 189 of 1945/6, para. 44.
[156] Jennings, p. 122.
[157] Jennings, pp. 124–5.
[158] Jennings, pp. 131–2.
[159] H.C. Deb. c. 1330, 16th March 1960.
[160] *The Times*, 2nd June 1960.
[161] Muir, p. 224.
[162] H.C. 161 of 1930/1, Q. 133, 323.
[163] H.C. 92 of 1958/59, p. 174n.
[164] Jennings, *op. cit*. p. 133.
[165] H.C. 92 of 1958/59, para. 9.
[166] *ibid*. Q. 678; p. 208.
[167] *ibid*. p. 4.
[168] *ibid*. p. 196.
[169] *ibid*. Q. 1085.
[170] Einzig, pp. 12, 326–7.
[171] H.C. 92 of 1958/59, pp. 15–16.
[172] *ibid*. para. 43.

[173] *Manchester Guardian*, 22nd July 1957.

[174] H.C. Deb, 619, c. 1342.

[175] Under 'Legislation', section (*c*) below.

[176] Proposals which affect the procedure for Private Members' Bills are considered later, in Chapter IV.

[177] H.C. 161 of 1930/1, pp. 311–2; and *Political Quarterly*, Vol. IV, 1933, pp. 467–81.

[178] H.C. 92 of 1958/9, p. 2.

[179] *Political Quarterly*, Vol. I, 1930.

[180] Parliament sometimes allows this to occur in the case of Private Bills, but never with Public Bills.

[181] *Contemporary Review*, Vol. CXLIII, February 1933.

[182] Pollard: *How to Reform Parliament*, 1944.

[183] H.C. 161 of 1930/31, Q. 1065.

[184] *Political Quarterly*, Vol. II, 1931, pp. 305ff.

[185] H.C. 161 of 1930/31, Q. 2514.

[186] *Political Quarterly*, Vol. V, 1934.

[187] *English Review*, Vol. LXI, pp. 657–64.

[188] Greaves, pp. 42–4.

[189] *An Introduction to the Procedure of the House of Commons*, 3rd ed. 1958, p. 131.

[190] H.C. 92 of 1958/9, para. 20.

[191] H.C. Deb. 617, c. 121.

[192] H.C. Deb. 617, cs. 158–62.

[193] H.C. 161 of 1930/1, p. 284.

[194] Jennings, p. 73.

[195] H.C. Deb. 400, cs. 1089–90.

[196] Jennings, pp. 69–70.

[197] Pollard: *op. cit.* p. 43.

[198] *Political Quarterly*, Vol. I, 1930.

[199] H.C. 310 of 1952/3, p. xxiv.

[200] Jennings, pp. 61–3.

[201] Muir, p. 210.

[202] *Political Quarterly*, Vol. V, pp. 469–79.

[203] Jennings, pp. 73–7. Some of the objections which Jennings raised have been obviated by subsequent changes in Standing Orders. His Standing Committee on Finance is mentioned in section (*a*) of this chapter.

[204] H.C. 92 of 1958/9, p. 16.

[205] H.C. 161 of 1930/1, Q. 258.

[206] Motion, 18th December 1946.

[207] H.C. 161 of 1930/1, Q. 35.

[208] H.C. Deb. 557, c. 1322.

[209] *Parliamentary Affairs*, Vol. VI, 1952–3, pp. 165–72.

[210] Jennings, p. 79

[211] *The Machinery of Government*, O.U.P. 1945.

[212] *Parliamentary Affairs*, Vol. VI, 1952–3, pp. 165–72.

[213] H.C. 161 of 1930/1, p. 174.

[214] *ibid.* p. 443.

[215] H.C. 92 of 1958/9, para. 6, Q. 1089, 1122.

[216] H.C. 161 of 1930/1, p. 442.

[217] The use of Committees to consider a Department's Estimates is considered in section (*a*) of this chapter.

[218] H.C. 189 of 1945/6, pp. 39–42.
[219] H.C. 92 of 1958/9, para. 13; and pp. 3–4.
[220] See pp. 43–55 above.
[221] Jennings, p. 85.
[222] *Parliamentary Affairs*, Vol. XI, No. 3.
[223] *ibid.* Vol. VI, pp. 165–72.
[224] Jennings, pp. 86–90.
[225] *The Fortnightly*, Vol. CLXI, pp. 425–32.
[226] Jennings, p. 93.
[227] Now S.O. No. 10.
[228] *Parliamentary Affairs*, Vol. XI, No. 3.
[229] *Parliamentary Affairs*, Vol. XI, No. 3.
[230] H.C. 92 of 1958/9, para. 7.
[231] H.C. 161 of 1930/1, p. 330.
[232] H.C. Deb. 430, cs. 1102–30.
[233] H.C. 161 of 1930/1, Q. 949.
[234] H.C. 189 of 1945/6, p. 43
[235] In a memorandum (unpublished) to the Select Committee on Procedure in 1945.
[236] H.C. 92 of 1958/9, Q. 1045.
[237] *ibid.* para. 10.
[238] *op. cit.* pp. 42–4.
[239] Pollard, p. 43.
[240] Jennings, pp. 107–8.
[241] It seems probable that Jennings was thinking of Recommittal (when some Clauses might be debated), rather than Report (when there is no opportunity for debating individual Clauses).
[242] H.C. 161 of 1930/1, p. 443.
[243] Stewart: *The British Approach to Politics*, 3rd revised ed., 1955, p. 117.
[244] H.C. 161 of 1930/1, p. 174. This reverses the emphasis which the House at present places on the relative effectiveness of a Committee stage in Standing Committee and on the floor of the House. For if a bill is unamended in Committee of the Whole House, it can go for Third Reading without a Report stage; but a bill unamended in a Standing Committee *must* still go for a Report stage on the floor of the House.
[245] *ibid.* p. 155.
[246] H.C. 92 of 1958/9, para. 11.
[247] H.C. Deb. 617, cs. 157, 181–2.
[248] *Introduction to the Procedure of the House of Commons*, 3rd ed., 1958, p. 296.
[249] Muir, p. 213.
[250] Lord Campion, p. 296.
[251] H.C. 139 of 1954/5.
[252] *ibid.* paras. 60–5, 73, 74.
[253] H.C. 92 of 1958/9, para. 23.
[254] H.C. 161 of 1930/1, Qs. 175, 333, 1527.
[255] H.C. 92 of 1958/9, Q. 1045.
[256] *Crossbow*, Vol. 4, No. 10, p. 12.
[257] e.g. H.C. Deb. 574, cs. 1525ff.
[258] Motions, 18th November 1952, 22nd April 1953, 19th June 1956, and 22nd November 1956.

[259] H.C. Deb. 581, c. 669–771 *passim*; 557, c. 1293–352 *passim*; 510, c. 529 *et seq.*
[260] M. Lindsay: *The Times*, 28th December 1957.
[261] H.C. 92 of 1958/9, pp. 6–7; and para. 24, pp. 39–42.
[262] H.C. Deb. 617, c. 165.
[263] H.C. Deb. 510, cs. 529ff, and H.C. 92 of 1958/9, p. 3 and Q. 667.
[264] e.g. H.C. Deb. 510, c. 533.
[265] II.C. 92 of 1958/9, pp. 8–9.
[266] Muir pp. 206–7.
[267] H.C. Deb. 577, c. 782.
[268] H.C. Deb. 347, c. 2500–4.
[269] H.C. 161 of 1930/1, Q. 574–6.
[270] H.C. Deb. 434, c. 1500–6.
[271] H.C. Deb. 459, c. 1621.
[272] See H.C. Deb. 510, c. 547 (mentioned in a speech by A. Greenwood).
[273] H.C. 92 of 1958/9, para. 27.
[274] H.C. 189 of 1945/6, p. 45.
[275] H.C. 92 of 1958/9, p. 6.
[276] H.C. Deb. 577, c. 781–2.
[277] H.C. 92 of 1958/9, para. 27.
[278] e.g. H.C. 161 of 1930/1, Q. 573; Early day motion No. 46, Session 1959/60.
[279] H.C. Deb. 581, c. 694.
[280] See H. C. Deb. 315, c. 25.
[281] H.C. Deb. 369, c. 1148; 459, c. 1616–28; 510, c. 541.
[282] c.g. H.C. Deb. 459, cs. 1616–28.
[283] H.C. Deb. 617, c. 41.
[284] H.C. Deb. 510, c. 573–4.
[285] e.g. H.C. Deb. 310, c. 1625–6.
[286] H.C. Deb. 510, c. 602.
[287] e.g. H.C. Deb. 266, c. 1339; 347, c. 2500–4.
[288] H.C. 189 of 1945/6, para 59. For a full description of the difficulties, see para 31 of the Appendix to that Report.
[289] H.C. Deb. 459, 1624.
[290] H.C. Deb. 266, c. 1340.
[291] H.C. 92 of 1958/9, Q. 535.
[292] H.C. Deb. 617, c. 110.
[293] H.C. Deb. 617, c. 138.
[294] H.C. Deb. 310, c. 1625–6.
[295] e.g. H.C. Deb. 557, c. 1334.
[296] H.C. 92 of 1958/9, para. 55.
[297] Motion, 1st May 1947.
[298] H.C. Deb. 504, c. 397.
[299] H.C. Deb. 307, c. 300–2; 459, c. 1618.
[300] H.C. Deb. 272, c. 61–2.
[301] H.C. Deb. 266, c. 1339.
[302] H.C. Deb. 443, c. 1584–6.
[303] H.C. Deb. 617, c.111
[304] H.C. Deb. 434, cs. 1500–6 (raised by Ellis Smith and others.)
[305] *ibid.*
[306] H.C. Deb. 307, cs. 300–2.
[307] e.g. Motion, 24th November 1956.
[308] e.g. H.C. Deb. 347, cs. 2500–4.

[309] H.C. 92 of 1958/9, para. 29.

[310] H.C. Deb. 617, col. 164–5.

[311] For a full exposition of the subject see P. Howarth: *Questions in the House*, Bodley Head, 1956.

[312] H.C. 161 of 1930/1, p. 443.

[313] *ibid*. Q. 159, 1250.

[314] H.C. 332 of 1951/2.

[315] H.C. 161 of 1930/1, p. 64, p. 443. A member may now put down two starred Questions (i.e. Questions for oral answer) for a particular day, but any number of unstarred Questions (i.e., Questions for written answer) which must be answered within the week.

[316] H.C. Deb. 615, c. 1463.

[317] H.C. 161 of 1930/1, Q. 2500.

[318] H.C. 129 of 1931/2, p. 14.

[319] H.C. 92 of 1958/9, Q. 1067.

[320] H.C. Deb. 510, c. 567.

[321] H.C. 92 of 1958/9, para. 41.

[322] *ibid*. para 40.

[323] H.C. Deb. 418, c. 1713.

[324] Motion, 10th July 1958; and H.C. Deb. 612, cs. 67–8.

[325] H.C. Deb. 615, cs. 175–8.

[326] H.C. 161 of 1930/1, p. 444.

[327] *ibid*. p. 443, Q. 159, 605.

[328] H.C. Deb. 557, c. 1332.

[329] Motion, 14th March 1949.

[330] H.C. 92 of 1958/9, para. 42.

[331] *ibid*. pp. 9–10.

[332] H.C. 161 of 1930/1, p. 172.

[333] *Political Quarterly*, Vol. 1, 1930, pp. 351–67.

[334] H.C. 58 of 1945/6, para. 3.

[335] H.C. 92 of 1958/9, para. 38.

[336] *The Times*, 25th April 1960.

[337] Heinemann, Ltd. 1932, p. 573.

[338] Ross, *Parliamentary Representation*, p. 9.

[339] e.g. cf. *The Times*, 28th December 1957.

[340] H.C. 58 of 1945/6, p. 50. It should be pointed out that this was at the start of a new Parliament which included a high proportion of new members; as the Division Clerks familiarized themselves with the new faces, the time was likely to drop to nine minutes (Q.1687).

[341] H.C. 161 of 1930/1, Q. 339; and echoed by C. Davies, H.C. Deb, 510, c. 581.

[342] Morrison, p. 215.

[343] H.C. 92 of 1958/9, Q. 1046.

[344] H.C. 58 of 1945/6, pp. 50–2.

[345] H.C. 92 of 1958/9, para. 32; pp. 218–223.

[346] *ibid*. p. 223; Q. 784.

[347] 1st December 1952.

[348] e.g. by Hinchingbrooke, H.C. Deb. 557, c. 1322.

[349] H.C. Deb. 510, c. 561.

[350] Acland, p. 170.

[351] H.C. 92 of 1958/9, para. 37; and Q. 815.

[352] H.C. Deb. 617, cs. 104–5.

[353] e.g. Hollis, *Parliamentary Affairs*, Vol. VI, pp. 165–72.
[354] H. Hynd, H.C. Deb. 510, c. 541.
[355] H.C. Deb. 510, c. 552.
[356] e.g. H.C. Deb. 581, c. 752; and the *Observer*, 14th December 1958.
[357] H.C. 161 of 1930/1, p. 115.
[358] S.O. No. 34; see H.C. 58 of 1945/6, p. 51.
[359] H. Hynd, H.C. Deb. 510, c. 541.
[360] *Crossbow*, Vol. 4, No. 10, pp. 11–13.
[361] H.C. 92 of 1958/59, p. 6; and Q. 653–4, paras. 31, 34.
[362] Delargy; H.C. Deb. 581, c. 747; and Bevan, H.C. Deb. 400, c. 1108.
[363] H.C. 92 of 1958/9, Q. 143–7.
[364] H.C. Deb. 617, c. 108.
[365] Hinchingbrooke, H.C. Deb. 557, c. 1322.
[366] H.C. 92 of 1958/9, para. 16; and Q. 1162.
[367] H.C. Deb. 557, c. 1322. The time has since been increased to four minutes.
[368] de Freitas; H.C. Deb. 510, c. 568.
[369] C. Davies; H.C. Deb. 510, c. 579.
[370] Acland, p. 171.
[371] H.C. Deb. 617, cs. 70–2.
[372] Wedgwood Benn, H.C. Deb. 557, c. 1333; and 581, cs. 681–2.
[373] de Freitas, H.C. Deb. 581, c. 696; and H.C. 92 of 1958/9, para 53.
[374] *Manchester Guardian*, 1st December 1952.
[375] H.C. 92 of 1958/9, para. 37, p. xlvi.
[376] Wedgwood Benn, H.C. Deb. 557, c. 1335; and 581, c. 683.
[377] Boyle, H.C. Deb. 510, c.588.
[378] Keeling, H.C. Deb. 508, c. 628.
[379] H.C. 92 of 1958/9, p. lii.
[380] Lord Winterton, H.C. Deb. 400, c. 1074–6.
[381] Bevan, H. C. Deb. 400, c. 1096; and 443, c. 1569; see also Jennings, p. 138 and an article by H. V. Wiseman in *Parliamentary Affairs*, Vol. XII, Nos. 3 and 4, pp. 377–91.
[382] H.C. 92 of 1958/9, p. 12, para. 34.
[383] H.C. Deb. 617, c. 161–4.
[384] Hynd: H.C. Deb. 510, c. 542.
[385] Jennings, p. 165.
[386] Einzig, p. 331.

IV

The Party System in Parliament

(*a*) THE NEED FOR POLITICAL PARTIES

It is perfectly in order to distinguish between two ways of viewing the whole question of parliamentary reform.[1] There is, on the one hand, the comparatively restricted field of parliamentary procedure proper, such as that covered by the latest Select Committee in its report.[2] The proposals made therein may not have gone as far as many critics would have wished.[3] But the Select Committee was bound by its terms of reference to confine itself to the specifically defined task of suggesting how the House of Commons, *as it is*, might be made to function more effectively. The alternative approach is to consider every factor, large and small, which affects the working of Parliament as the central point of the country's governmental system. Electoral reform, for example, demands these broader terms of reference if it is to be properly discussed. Similarly, any detailed examination of the supposed merits and defects of the party system must fall into this second, wider category.

However true it may be that political parties, as we know them to-day in their parliamentary context, just grew whilst nobody was looking, their importance is now as great as it is incontestable.[4] A galaxy of illustrious parliamentarians from Burke by way of Disraeli to Winston Churchill, have at some juncture testified not only to the importance but also to the desirability of party politics. 'I know of no equal force', declared Winston Churchill in the House of Commons over fifty years ago, 'which assures the stability of democratic institutions.'[5] Government exists for the benefit of the governed, but democracy in Lincoln's sense of

For Notes and References see pages 113–116

'Government by the People' is an impossible ideal. Twentieth-century Britain accepts political parties—bodies of individuals and affiliated organizations having similar views on leading issues and uniting in order to gain the power to apply their beliefs—as the best way of combining effective government with a reasonably democratic expression of the electorate's wishes.[6] Distinguished former Independent Members, such as Sir Alan Herbert, themselves subscribe to the above belief.[7] Michael Foot, who has lately had much to say against certain aspects of party discipline, concedes unreservedly that the disappearance of party politics would mean the death of democracy. A robust repudiation is needed, he continues, of those sneers which have aimed at making 'Party' a dirty word in the political dictionary.[8] Because of these practical advantages, none of the suggested reforms discussed below aims at the total abolition of parties, even supposing such a carnage to be possible. The answer to the question: 'Why have parties?' is quite simple: 'For convenience'.[9]

Contradictory though it may seem, this widespread acquiescence in the existence of such highly organized political bodies has been accompanied over the years by criticisms which, in volume and intensity, surpass those attacks levelled against all other aspects of parliamentary government. The explanation of this apparent paradox is not hard to find. The party system influences almost every ingredient of present-day British democracy. Hence, its real or imagined defects assume enhanced, far-flung significance because of their potential consequences. Since the system is held to be practically indispensable, its workings have been minutely examined and its supposed weaknesses pitilessly exposed.

(b) GOVERNMENT AND OPPOSITION

In British national government to-day the political scene is very often dominated by two great parties. The two-party system, remarked Sir Harold Nicolson at the Caxton Hall on 14th March 1946, is illogical and indefensible—but it is the best means of running representative institutions.[10] In like vein, Sir Ernest Barker speaks of the struggle for power between two parties as the salt of British democracy.[11] The two-party system, in short, has its protagonists. But others have not been slow to emphasize its dangers. Maurice Duverger claims that, although this country *officially* maintains a parliamentary system (that is, a system with modified separation of powers, Cabinet and Parliament each specializing in a particular function), *in practice* Parliament and Government are like two machines driven by the same motor—the party in power. The Opposition provides the alternative (party) motor.[12] Muir points out that an elector is frequently confronted with a choice between two parties; he appreciates that no other party can possibly form a Government,[13] yet he may not agree with the fundamental policies of either alternative.[14] It remains for him to vote for the lesser of two evils, to 'waste' his vote on another candidate whose hopes of success are negligible, or to abstain. This sort of drawback appears even more pernicious to those who believe that the differences between the two main contesting parties are less great than would appear at first sight. Not many are as bitter as Belloc and Cecil Chesterton, who spoke of 'collusion' between the two front benches, from which the Speaker himself was not exempt.[15] Yet a leading article in *The Times* commented harshly on a House of Commons containing 'far too many little men' and engaging in 'desperate fighting over things that do not matter'.[16] Fulford, putting the Liberal case, refers to 'two monstrous, inhuman party political machines' existing only to smash each other.[17] Much snapping and snarling goes on, he asserts, over comparative trifles.[18] R. T. McKenzie, at the close of his lengthy survey, pictures 'two great monolithic structures' facing each other in the Commons, debating furiously the comparatively minor issues which divide them.[19] The condition of Parliament's impotence, writes Hollis, is the two-party system.[20] If one accepts that these grave indictments are not wholly false, then Crossman's complaint that Cabinet government is a polite title for alternating party oligarchy cannot be lightly dismissed.[21]

The proposals for remedying such serious charges (assuming for the moment they are not groundless) vary considerably in type and magnitude. The most far-reaching suggestion, perhaps, is that party government should be replaced by Coalition government—the parties would not disappear, but the best men from all parties would take office under an accepted leader. The experience of the war years is plainly discernible here. Laski says that the Asquith and Lloyd George Coalitions of 1915 and 1916 respectively were essential contributions towards ultimate victory in 1918, and he refers to the inspiring change in the spirit of the whole nation when the Labour Party agreed to serve under Churchill in May 1940.[22] But the same author goes on to illustrate at some length that such Coalitions are highly unsatisfactory in time of peace;[23] the Coalition of 1931 he condemns as a dangerous threat to parliamentary institutions.[24] An administration of this sort blurs responsibility, prevents issues being clearly defined, and hampers their realistic discussion.[25] Many others argue cogently against peace-time Coalitions on the grounds that the quintessential virtue of parliamentary democracy depends upon the full freedom of articulate constitutional opposition.[26] 'Mr. Ramsay MacDonald's conception of the ideal Parliament as a Council of State in which the Opposition co-operate with the Government for the common good', concludes Laski, 'seems to me to come near to opening the door to the one-party state'. And, as Sir Ernest Barker has pointed out, 'party uses its giant's strength most like a giant when it stands solitary'.[27] Broadly speaking, then, Disraeli was an accurate prophet when he said in 1852 that 'England does not love Coalitions'.

Following his highly critical survey of the two-party system, Muir[28] advocates Minority Government as desirable, since it compels the party forming the Government to follow policies which are not totally unacceptable to all the other major parties represented in the Commons. Undeniably, the task which faces a party not disposing of an overall majority, yet setting out to legislate as a Minority Government, is difficult. But Muir does not consider the task impossible, providing the following conditions obtain:

(a) A Minority Ministry must accept that it cannot hope to carry out measures for which it has no support outside its own party. In other words, it is powerless to effect policies for which there is not a majority of support in the country as a whole.

(b) Parties outside the Government must not devote themselves primarily and exclusively to opposing the Government. Free criticism would not be barred, but the current Ministry would be afforded 'reasonable facilities' to pursue its policies, provided these were not generally unacceptable.

(c) In return for this concession, the Minority Government must allow greater freedom of debate in the Commons, and accept a greater amount of amendments to its Bills.

(d) Nothing less than a vital issue of principle should prompt the Government to threaten resignation.

(e) The most important of all conditions, if effective administration is to take place under a balance of parties, is that a Minority Government should have *no* right to claim a dissolution. If the Ministry's resignation is felt to be imperative, then Parliament should embody its majority decision in an Humble Address to the Crown.[29]

Given the establishment of these very considerable understandings or conventions, Muir postulates that parliamentary government 'can work very well in a condition of balanced parties: not only so, but an opportunity will be opened for the House of Commons to perform its true, but long abdicated, functions of criticism and control'.[30] Ross also has something to say in favour of Minority Government—the 'bloated majorities' of the two great parties are not conducive to healthy government.[31] This whole question is, of course, intimately associated with the campaign for the introduction in this country of Proportional Representation—under this latter electoral system, it might easily happen that no party would obtain an absolute majority in the House. Muir goes further, postulating such electoral reform as essential to the long-term success of Minority Government.[32] But critics of this form of administration heavily outnumber those who favour it. Barker points out that such a system might easily lead to the secret 'backstairs' tyranny of a cabal which would unite the leaders of several parties in an interested coalition—a cabal which would control both the nominal Government and the legislative body. Perhaps, too, the opportunity of pressing a Minority Government for concessions might tempt the parties not in power to demand their own pound of flesh, to the detriment of both Executive and

Parliament.[33] Bulmer-Thomas similarly emphasizes the potential menace of secret inter-party negotiations under such a system: not only is this inherently vicious, but the election promises of the various parties would become meaningless.[34] Elections leading to Minority Government, in fact, would play virtually no part in deciding the eventual policy of the administration. Responsible, effective rule on behalf of the people would be considerably weakened.[35] Above all, Minority Government could well lead to some sort of Coalition; the arguments against this last possibility have been mentioned.

Many of those who prefer the two-party system to the alternatives discussed above, nevertheless concede that the debates staged on the floor of the House between the two main opposing factions have lost a great deal of their former significance. It is sometimes alleged that the now firmly established practice of holding private party meetings at Westminster, when affairs of national import are discussed behind closed doors, is a major cause of this decline. Michael Foot has recently claimed that 'the higher the party meeting rises on the see-saw, the lower sinks the Commons'.[36] The fact that decisions reached behind closed doors are often regarded by the parties as critical and binding, leads Foot to his melancholy pen-portrait of a House of Commons where two well-whipped forces confront each other in formal, pre-arranged combat. Speeches of Gladstonian power or Disraelite piquancy are unlikely to shift a single vote.[37] Hollis inveighs with comparable vigour against 'the very disgraceful truth' that the private Member, though relatively impotent in the Chamber, can influence the policy of his party (and often of the Government) at some secret meeting.[38] Foot's proposed remedy is simple: if votes have to be taken at private gatherings, then the results should not be binding on a Member's conduct in the House. An M.P. would, as a result, be fully answerable to the country and his constituents for his public speeches and/or votes.[39] The controversial nature of such a suggestion scarcely requires emphasizing. Beyond doubt, the potential consequences of diminishing in this way the status of the private party meeting could strike at the very heart of the party system, so dependent on unity for its continuing success. Internal feuds, once exposed to open view, would be exploited mercilessly by political opponents. Richards writes that 'the repeated inability of Liberal Members since 1916 to vote together in the same division lobby has done much to accelerate the decline of their Party'.[40] Granted the existing pattern of our political life, observes the same author, it is 'idealistic' to suppose that the claims of party loyalty will be much diminished.[41]

The movement for the compulsory publication of political parties' accounts has attracted considerable attention for many years. The matter was raised anew in a debate on Procedure on 26th May 1944, when King-Hall suggested that the funds of political parties should be opened to public inspection. On 15th December 1949, Geoffrey Bing moved 'that ... political parties, and all other organizations having political action as one of their aims, should publish annually full and adequate statements of their accounts'.[42] The principal point of this proposal, as regards parliamentary reform, is that the vital financing of those political organizations competing for the electors' support should be open to proper public investigation, criticism and control. The whole question of political expenditure was again debated in the Commons on 21st July 1960, when the Labour Party called for an Inquiry into the matter. P. Gordon-Walker, moving the amendment, quoted from *The Times* of 9th June 1960:

> In so far as the law regulating election expenses is supposed to set a reasonable limit to the electeering budgets of political parties so as to cancel the undue advantage of wealth, the law is obviously defective.

Butler and Rose have pointed out that, since people now tend to vote for a party rather than for a candidate, there is nothing in the law to prevent parties or interested organizations from intervening on a national scale during and before the electoral campaign.[43] They concluded that if the necessity for legislation regarding control of political expenditure had still to be proved, the case for an investigation into the situation nevertheless appeared overwhelming.

Protagonists of the two-party system emphasize consistently the importance of an articulate, effective Opposition. Parliamentary democracy would falter without it: the Heaven of the Right is the Hell of the Left, observes Jennings, and it is only in totalitarian states that the populace can be made to exclaim 'Excelsior!' whether the Government moves forwards or backwards (or in both directions at the same time).[44] It is also now an accepted fact that the Opposition's function is constructive as well as destructive. But the argument is sometimes advanced that the two-party system would work better if the official Opposition were informed earlier, and more fully, of all major Government policies. Acland contends that the principal party not in power should be allowed representatives *within* the State Departments. 'Shadow Ministers' privileged in this way would not be permitted to monopolize the precious time of senior officials, but their inevitably improved knowledge of Government matters would transform democratic criticism into an effective reality. The Civil Service, concludes Acland, belongs to the nation, not to the Government.[45] The principle underlying such a suggestion is not new, but the question seems to have come to a head in recent years. According to Laski, speaking in 1950, 'it is not easy to believe that the House of Commons has been honestly informed of the facts which have led to its approval of policies which have concerned grave issues like those of Abyssinia, Spain, Italy, Greece, Germany and Russia; and not without skill, it has been manœuvred into something like an organized silence over the atomic bomb and the present state of our military commitments'.[46] The gravity of the accusation is clear. The charge is not infrequently levelled against the party in power, as it was, for example, during debates on the Suez crisis. Hollis, in his pamphlet *Has Parliament a Future?* deplores the frequency with which Government and Opposition agree *not* to debate a matter under discussion elsewhere. This detracted from Parliament's efficiency. As distinct from Acland's and Hollis's suggestions, many informed critics would like to see all-party Committees of the House of Commons set up to investigate various aspects of national affairs; such Committees would always contain Opposition Members, who would thus be able to investigate, intimately and in detail, the particular aspect of Government policy allotted to their Committee.[47] These different suggestions underline the generally accepted idea that Parliamentary democracy needs an active, informed Opposition if it is to continue to flourish under the aegis of the party system. It has been said that no Government can be long secure without a formidable Opposition; the fact that the Government pays the Leader of the Opposition an official salary, testifies to the unanimous acceptance of the latter body's importance.[48]

(c) THE PRIVATE MEMBER AND HIS PARTY

The influence of political parties in Parliament is by no means confined to the Government and Opposition, conceived of as two organized bodies facing each other in the House of Commons. Indeed, the most substantial volume of recent criticism has been directed at the pressure and discipline exerted on the individual Member by his or her own party. The comparative decline in the Private Member's independence and initiative is regarded by many as a serious, deplorable feature of modern politics. Describing the individual as the obedient servant of the party machine, Hollis has suggested that it would be simpler (and certainly more economical) if a flock of tame sheep, kept conveniently at hand, were guided through Westminster's division lobbies in appropriate numbers at agreed times.[49] Hollis's pessimistic view of the situation is echoed less spectacularly by other informed observers. R. T. McKenzie feels that genuine political dissent is unduly discouraged by the parties' inflexibility;[50] Bulmer-Thomas warns that fewer men of ability will enter Parliament if the present restrictions on free speech continue.[51] Criticism of this kind is not restricted to the post-war years, but it has certainly come to the forefront following the abolition of university constituencies by the 1948 Representation of the People Act.[52] Since then, the one Independent candidate to be *elected* to Parliament has been Sir David Robertson—and he, himself a former Conservative, was not opposed by a Conservative candidate.[53] Generally speaking, therefore, the contention that mass electorates are fatal to the politically unorthodox is justified.[54] Voters are swayed by national issues rather than by personalities. A candidate, in short, depends on his party affiliations. Given this post-war state of affairs, the independence or otherwise of an M.P. *within* his party is a matter of extreme importance—for honest, informed political dissent is accepted without question as the life-blood of Parliamentary democracy.[55] As Crossman emphasizes, if the Member is responsible primarily to his party, not to his electors, then a

Government cannot be wholly responsible to the House of Commons.[56] How, then, can 'honest political dissent' be best encouraged?

Acland has suggested that all Members of the Commons should be guaranteed a reasonable income for life, even when no longer serving at Westminster.[57] The consequence of such comparative security would be that men and women of modest means would be more willing to speak out against their party's policy, since an enforced or voluntary farewell to Westminster would no longer incur extreme financial hardship. Ross advocates that a Member, on giving up or losing his seat, should receive for a 'limited time' that part of his remuneration ranking as salary. This 'limited time' would not exceed his previous active service in the Commons, and would in no case be longer than three years. A person's private income would also have to be considered before an award of this type was made.[58] An inquiry into the operation of the House of Commons Members' Fund was undertaken by the Select Committee on Members' Expenses which reported in 1953-54, and which put forward a suggestion for a non-contributory pensions scheme.[59] The Committee argued in favour of its proposal (which would of necessity impose upon the taxpayer) that M.P.s were servants of the public—a capricious employer with the right to dismiss them without ceremony.[60] The scheme as such was not implemented, although on 22nd February 1957 it was announced that an annual Government contribution of ten thousand pounds would be made to the Members' Fund. This plea for some financial security for former M.P.s has had its opponents. An article in *The Times*, for instance, declared categorically that a Member of Parliament who asks for security in his career is seeking a prize to which freely elected representatives were not entitled.[61] Lady Tweedsmuir has observed: 'Whatever any of us may feel about the necessity for pensions, for example, for past Members of this House . . . all of us who sit in the House now knew exactly the terms and conditions of service and the risks to our dependents when we decided to stand for Parliament'.[62] Fears that improved financial security might attract more 'professional politicians' to Parliament have also been voiced on a number of occasions. But there seems now to be general recognition of the need for a fairly wide sprinkling of 'full-time' M.P.s—however artificial or invidious that term may sound.[63] As Richards has pointed out, the introduction of payment to Members as far back as 1911 has led inevitably to the presence in Parliament of men without private means.[64] Such Members, moreover, often make sacrifices to serve in the Commons. Whilst any discussions of the country's moral obligations in the matter would be out of place here, the popularity of the argument that some financial security as regards his future might well lead to a Member's greater independence within his party is undeniable. For example, following criticism in *The Times* of the proposal for non-contributory pensions,[65] both Attlee and Acland wrote letters in defence of some such scheme.[66]

The recommendations of the Select Committee regarding a non-contributory scheme for Members' pensions, mentioned in the preceding paragraph, were the subject of a free vote in the Commons on 24th May 1954. This leads us to another proposal aimed at increasing Private Members' independence: there should be more free votes. Grimond has said that Parliament ought to be 'less dragooned on every issue by the Whips';[67] Hollis has also campaigned assiduously for relaxed discipline of this sort. Foot claims that dignity, spontaneity, suspense, surprise and significance will return to Commons debates if more free votes are permitted: the division lobby will no longer be a 'corridor of humiliation' where the M.P. must wear the badge of his tribe.[68] It is true that more free votes would entail extra work, sharper headaches and, possibly, confusion of the issues as far as the Government is concerned. In particular, Ministers can expect trouble if they decline to follow a clear-cut verdict reached by the House without the assistance of the Whips.[69] Some would simply say that such a price was well worth paying. Others, more mindful of the Government's problems, suggest that more free votes would be possible if the result were not necessarily regarded as a vote of confidence. Cripps said in 1933 that unless the Cabinet threatened to resign less regularly the 'take it or leave it' atmosphere engendered in the Chamber would render discussion abortive.[70] In like vein, Captain Cunningham-Reid wanted to see a Government resign only if defeated on a vote of censure, which would *follow* a Government defeat in the lobbies.[71] Whether this latter proposal is accepted or not, keen advocates of increased free-voting argue that their proposals would not render a Government's task impossible.

'Honest political dissent' need not be incompatible with basic loyalty to one's party, and few Members would abuse their freedom since they must face their electors at regular intervals. The Government backbencher with hopes of office would have added reasons for treating such liberty with respect and restraint. It is probably true that convinced supporters of a stable Executive would still claim that free votes should remain an occasional luxury, whilst no Government is itself likely to encourage such a policy.[72] Nevertheless, the charges levelled against excessive 'dragooning' in the division lobbies, whether completely justified or not, have been sufficiently frequent and outspoken of late to merit serious attention being paid to the question.

Bulmer-Thomas, supporting the plea for more free votes and fewer questions of confidence, adds that tolerance of personal dissent within the party should be accompanied by similar tolerance on the part of an M.P.'s constituency organization: 'An executive committee which is always brooding over the Member's speeches, passing resolutions of censure on his votes, and threatening him with the withdrawal of support at the next election is doing a great disservice to representative government.'[73] The spectacular issue as to whether a Member is a representative or a delegate is involved here. Without debating the merits or defects of Burke's classic answer to the question, we may fairly say that the Suez crisis— which provoked definitive ruptures between several M.P.s and their constituency organizations—revealed substantial support for the eighteenth-century statesman's words to his electors at Bristol. 'Your *representative*', Burke had said, 'owes you, not his industry only, but his judgement, and he betrays, instead of serving you, if he sacrifices it to your opinion.'[74] King-Hall, in the debate on Procedure of 26th May 1944, detected a tendency that the electorate, more and more, wanted to feel that their *representatives* had minds of their own, and were not 'perambulating rubber stamps'. In a speech to his constituency association, Nigel Nicolson declined in public an invitation to resign his seat because he had opposed his Party's policy in the Suez affair.[75] Shortly afterwards, Nicolson published in *People and Parliament* his own account of the quarrel between his constituency organization and himself; in support of his views, he quoted Bagehot's axiom that constituency government is the precise opposite of parliamentary government,[76] and noted

Amery's preference for 'democracy by consent and not by delegation; government of the people, for the people, with but not by the people'.[77] The impression derived from this book is that party discipline can on occasions be wielded more firmly by the constituency associations than by the Whips at Westminster.[78] This was but one of several similar clashes between Members and their constituencies during 1956/7, and Fulford, in his Ramsay Muir Memorial Lecture at Oxford on 4th August 1957, concluded that the power of local political organizations had increased enormously of late, and ought to be diminished. How are the perils of excessive 'constituency government' to be avoided? First, a number of practical suggestions have been made concerning the selection of candidates by local associations: these proposals have been considered in an earlier chapter.[79] The second safeguard put forward is of a more general, abstract kind. If accepted, it would involve the acceptance locally of the principle that a Member of Parliament is not his electors' 'delegate', but their 'representative' in Burke's sense of the word. The Member would thus have the acknowledged right to speak against his party *in exceptional circumstances*. This last proviso is important—for few would deny that electors rightly attach significance to a party's being sufficiently united in order to form an effective Government or Opposition.[80] There is one more reason why a Member should not lightly go against his constituents' known wishes: local Party workers, mostly unpaid, toil hard and selflessly to support his candidature, and quite naturally expect loyalty from their elected representative as their just recompense.

(d) PRIVATE MEMBERS' TIME

Proposals to increase the independence and effectiveness of the Private Member fall into two broad categories. One of these categories—the right of an individual to express his personal views, even if they clash with his Party's official policy—has now been considered. The other broad type of proposed reform relates to the actual opportunities of back-benchers to make their presence felt in Parliament. That such opportunities have been seriously curtailed over the past hundred years is a well-known fact,[81] and suggestions to prevent the 'threatened eclipse'[82] of the individual

Member's initiative have acquired a definite sense of urgency. The proper place for the consideration of the majority of these proposals is in the chapter devoted to 'Procedure' (Chapter III). Those concerning Private Members' time, however, may perhaps be most usefully discussed here, if only because the subject is so typical of the constant struggle for time, opportunity and recognition waged to-day by the average back-bencher on both sides of the House. Of Private Members, Sir Alan Herbert said (to his prospective electors at East Harrow in December 1958): 'This is a fine and precious institution which must never be surrendered or belittled—especially the time set aside for Private Members' Bills.'

Although public interest fixes almost entirely on to Private Members' bills, it is as well to note that the House has lately allotted more time to Private Members' motions than to bills (the equivalent of twelve full days for motions, as against ten days for bills, each session).[83] Practice—as not infrequently happens in the House of Commons—is here at variance with the House's Standing Order,[84] which allows that normally there should be fourteen Fridays for bills each session, and seven Wednesdays for motions;[85] for the Standing Order is regularly waived, and replaced by a Sessional Order.

The threat to Private Members' time comes from three directions. There is, first, possible direct action by the Government, who can commandeer all or some of the available time for their own purposes when they feel that events justify it; this happened for example, in 1929–30, 1934–5, the war years, and the sessions from 1945–6 to 1947–8. In 1948–9 there were no motions, and in 1950 no bills.

A second and perhaps more sinister threat is the use Private Members can make of this time in order to bring forward official Opposition or Government business in disguise: Campion notes that Members often ballot in effect for the privilege of introducing a bill or moving a motion on behalf of their party.[86] And there can be said to be something cynical in the way in which a Government spokesman in the Lords, referring to a particular piece of future legislation, could say: 'All the necessary preparatory work . . . is being done to ensure that everything will be ready for the introduction of a Private Members' bill early next session.'[87]

Thirdly, there is the gravest threat of all; it is the apathy of Private Members themselves. On the motion to restore some Private Members' time after the war, the then Father of the House said: 'The House . . . has ceased to take any real practical interest in this matter.'[88] Nearly four years later, a former Leader of the House said that if Divisions on a Friday showed as small attendance as in the previous session, 'Private Members' business might very well fall into some contempt amongst the public outside.'[89]

Precedence on Private Members days is allotted by ballot. There is one ballot for bills early in the session, and members successful may choose on which of several allotted days they will move the Second Reading of their bills; a suggestion that this ballot should take place in the Session before (which proposal was supported by a draft Standing Order on the subject) was not taken up by the Procedure Committee in 1959.[90] Ballots for motions are held at various dates throughout the session; the successful Members are able to move motions of their choice on the appropriate day. The Select Committee on Procedure in 1946 recommended that one ballot should be held for both motions and bills;[91] winning Members could then choose to initiate whichever they preferred. The House, however, never gave effect to this proposal.

Private Members' motions, suggested Campion, could be given precedence according to the weight of support accorded to them by Members. Alternately, the ballot could decide between the motions proffered, rather than between the Members who put their names down.[92] Neither of these views commended itself to the Committee. Nor did they accept the Clerk's point that twenty half-day debates would prove more satisfactory than ten full days. They did not advocate reverting to the pre-war practice, where a Motion Day was divided into two, so that two short debates would invariably be held, instead of (possibly) one longer debate only. Other suggestions have been that the motions should be selected by a Committee, rather than by ballot; and that the ballot should be held, not as a choice between Members, but as a choice between known motions (possibly those motions placed on the Order Paper for debate on 'an early day').[93]

As to Private Members' bills, one point should be made clear from the outset. The procedure by which they pass into law is identical with that of all other public bills, their only peculiarity

109

being the way in which the best opportunities are ballotted for. It is to this peculiarity that most writers on the subject apply their minds; it is objected that the persistence of the eccentric is rewarded too often, so that too many Private Members' bills have a touch of the 'crank' about them.[94]

Campion suggested that Private Members' bills should be given precedence according to the amount of support they carried in the House; once a bill had been given precedence, no Member who had supported it could put his name to another bill for the remainder of the session.[95] This method (or its corollary, by which Members sign their name as objectors to a bill, and the bill with least objectors gets precedence) was considered by Pollard; his conclusion was that the best bills would still not necessarily get precedence in this way.[96]

The 1931 Procedure Committee recommended that, as the Session proceeds, the Committee of Selection might give precedence on Standing Committees to such bills as seemed likely to command general assent.[97] The House never gave effect to this, but Muir[98] and Michael Stewart[99] suggested that an all-party Committee should sit to select which of the Private Members' bills offered should have precedence. Bromhead also thought the idea worth considering.[100] But Pollard said it would be placing an invidious task upon the Committee.[101]

Laski suggested something which had a touch of both proposals: a bill with certain specified support (for example, twenty-five Members) could, if it involved law reform, be referred to a special Committee. This Committee would take evidence in public, and report to the House. If the report was favourable, the Government would be bound to allow time for the bill's further progress.[102]

Pollard's own view[103] was that the Speaker should, under certain stipulated conditions, certify bills as non-contentious. Such bills would then be given special facilities, perhaps on the lines of the Consolidation of Enactments (Procedure) Act, 1949.[104]

With this idea, we are getting away from the principle that the legislative process for a Private Members' bill should be the same as for any other public bill. Pollard goes even further from this principle when he postulates a lower quorum (twenty instead of forty) for the House when it is considering Private Members' business;[105] the Procedure Committee of 1958/9 rejected both this idea, and a proposal that it should be easier to carry the closure on a Private Members' day. They did, however, point out that the present practice allowed too little time for Private Members to prepare their bills, and recommended longer intervals between the initial stages of such bills.[106]

Finally, mention should be made of a suggestion by Ernest Davies that the Government might grant time for all Private Members' bills which had got Second Reading to make further progress even though all the allotted Fridays were used up.[107] Pollard believed that, after some general resolutions had been agreed to by the House, an Advisory Committee should consider the bill. If they reported favourably the Government should be bound to provide time for the bill.[108]

Bills and motions in Private Members' time do not, of course, exhaust the potentialities of the Private Member for taking part in the parliamentary game; the other resources are still there—questions, adjournment debates, the introduction of bills under other procedures, speeches on other people's proposals, etc. But the former present the only opportunity by which Members are actually encouraged to take action on matters in which they feel that a great issue is at stake here, that is why, for instance, Gordon has described Private Members' time as 'the precious initiative'.[109]

Conclusions

The volume and complexity of the work to be done at Westminster, combined with the existence of universal suffrage, make the party system an important and indispensable aspect of the Commons' present-day activities. The most zealous advocates of reform acknowledge the fact. A substantial amount of support for the two-party system is also evident, though such support is naturally by no means unanimous. Moreover, the criticisms and suggestions discussed in the preceding pages have of necessity focused attention on the real or supposed short-comings of the system, and it is only right and proper that very brief mention should be made, in concluding, of certain very positive advantages of the party system in Britain to-day. Apart from its eminent practicability,[110] the party machine, even as it exists to-day, does not completely stifle the initiative and independence of the Private

Member. The latter may not possess 'power'—that belongs to the Cabinet of the day—but he still has 'influence',[111] for it is of the essence of democracy that minority and even individual opinions must be heard and respected. Further, in times of crisis the Whips can lose their force. To the charge that it demands 'almost heroism' to defy one's Whips when voting,[112] many would retort that this is a quality not unknown to the British. Roy Jenkins has pointed out that freedom from the Whips, even if it could be granted, would not mean freedom from other 'pressures'[113]—the writer refers, no doubt, to Pressure Groups, the influence of which on Members of Parliament has been given some prominence in post-war years.[114]

These are but some of the strong arguments advanced in support of the part played by political parties in the Commons to-day. Nevertheless, it is still true that a vast body of current informed opinion does not regard their present influence as an unmixed blessing. The details of such criticisms and indictments, together with proposed remedies, have been discussed; it remains to speak of the general fear which underlies the bulk of those criticisms. Often this 'general fear' is implied rather than expressly stated. It is that the strong party system may eventually deprive Parliament of its vital role as the nation's safeguard against possible Executive dictatorship. One impartial observer who pointed *explicitly* to this threat was the late Lord Campion, sometime Clerk of the Commons: 'To their authority as servants of the King, wielding the powers of the prerogative, Ministers have added a second power, the power of Parliament itself. Through their command of a devoted party majority they have to a large extent in practice reversed the constitutional relation of the Executive to the House of Commons—as party leaders, they are in a position to control the controllers.'[115] Grimond, pointing out the relentless pressure on the Private Member of Government business, emphasizes the 'erosion of the defences once erected against the Executive'.[116] That the influence of the latter is too considerable, in the eyes of many, will emerge from the following chapter. It is already clear, however, that the preservation of some independence and personal initiative by the Private Member in the face of potential 'alternating Party oligarchy', 'constituency government' and other similar perils is regarded by many as quintessential if Parliament is to hold fast as the nation's watchdog. Speaking in support of increased opportunities for *Private* Members, one backbencher very recently declared: 'After all, Parliament was not intended simply as a machine to ratify measures proposed by the Executive. ... We (i.e. Private Members) have constitutional rights in this place which are important, rights for which men have died in the past and which we should not lightly sacrifice to the Executive. Much of the early history of this House, as all hon. Members know, is the struggle for the preservation of those rights against the eroding domination of the Executive. In stressing that, we are really only stressing *the rights and freedom of the nation as a whole.*'[117]

NOTES AND REFERENCES

[1] H. V. Wiseman: 'Parliamentary Reform' in *Parliamentary Affairs* Vol. XII, No. 2 (Spring 1959), p. 240.

[2] H.C. 92 of 1958/9.

[3] *Manchester Guardian*, 13th March 1959 (leading article: 'Parliament'). Crick similarly observes that the Select Committee report appears 'somewhat free from matters of general public interest', p. 24.

[4] W. Harrison: *The Government of Britain*, 1948, p. 50. This in no way invalidates the fact that political parties today are highly organized bodies.

[5] 31st March 1910.

[6] Curtis, pp. 18–20. R. T. McKenzie likewise emphasizes that policy cannot be initiated by the electorate as a whole.

[7] *Independent Member*, 1950, p. 337.

[8] M. Foot: *Parliament in Danger*, 1959, pp. 7–8.

[9] S. Gordon: *Our Parliament*, 5th ed., 1958, p. 80. The author, who points out that there is 'nothing sacred' about parties, goes on to say that they appear to suit the taste of the people, and that over a long term, the party system seems to be indispensable to the success of parliamentary government.

[10] Hansard Society Pamphlet, No. 2.

[11] Bailey (ed.): *The British Party System*, 1952, p. 198.

[12] M. Duverger: *Political Parties: Their Organization and Activity in the Modern State*, 2nd revised ed., 1959, p. 394. Lord Morrison of Lambeth has noted that one Labour Party publication referred to an Opposition Front-bencher as '*Minister* of — in the Shadow Cabinet'. (Morrison, pp. 349–50.)

[13] The Liberal Party manifesto at the 1959 General Election conceded to the elector; 'You will get a Tory or Socialist Government after this election . . . .'

[14] Muir, p. 145.

[15] In *The Party System*, 1911.

[16] 23rd December 1957, p. 7.

[17] *The Liberal Case*, 1960, pp. 18–19.

[18] *ibid.* pp. 25–6.

[19] McKenzie: *British Political Parties*, 1955, p. 586.

[20] H. Thomas (ed.): *The Establishment: A Symposium*, 1959, p. 186.

[21] *New Statesman*, 2nd April 1955, pp. 460–1.

[22] Laski, p. 57.

[23] *ibid.* pp. 58ff.

[24] *ibid.* p. 65.

[25] *ibid.* p. 71.

[26] e.g. (i) Jennings: *Parliament Must be Reformed*, 1941, pp. 15ff. (ii) Lord Samuel: 'The Party System and National Interest' (address to the Hansard Society at Denison House, 10th October 1945). (iii) Gaitskell: 'In Defence of Politics' (oration at Birkbeck College, December 1954).

[27] Barker: *Reflections on Government*, 1953, p. 212.

[28] Muir, Chap. IV, 'Political Parties and the Party System'.

[29] *ibid.* pp. 190–3.

[30] *ibid.* p. 193.

[31] *Parliamentary Representation*, pp. 225–9.

[32] Muir, pp. 193–4.

[33] In *The British Party System*, p. 196.

[34] Bulmer-Thomas, pp. 102–3.

[35] Butler: *The Electoral System in Great Britain 1918–1951*, 1953, pp. 188–9. This real or supposed defect of Minority Government is constantly emphasized by opponents of Proportional Representation—the electoral system most likely to lead to such a form of administration.

[36] Foot, p. 14.

[37] *ibid.*

[38] In *The Establishment*: *A Symposium*, p. 174.

[39] Foot, p. 27. Hollis has said, in similar vein: 'If the floor of the House should become the place of decision, then we shall have no need to worry about its prestige.' *Daily Telegraph*, 14th March 1959.

[40] Richards, p. 143.

[41] *ibid.* p. 254.

[42] H.C. Deb. 470, cs. 2972–3040. The Motion was carried by 213 votes to 104. Bing's case was based partly on his claim that, whereas the Liberal, Labour and Communist Parties published their accounts, the Conservative Party did not. c. 2972.

[43] Butler and Rose, Appendix 5.

[44] Jennings: *Parliament*, 2nd ed., 1957, p. 167.

[45] Acland, p. 171.

[46] Laski, p. 84.

[47] The proposals regarding such all-party Committees are considered more fully in Chapter III.

[48] 'The right honourable gentleman, the Member for South Leeds, is in his place on the Front Opposition Bench to exercise a function which is almost as important as the function of the right honourable gentleman (i.e. the Prime Minister) opposite.' Jennings: *op. cit.* p. 532.

[49] *Can Parliament Survive?*, pp. 64–5.

[50] McKenzie, pp. 585–6.

[51] Bulmer-Thomas, p. 271.

[52] See, for example, an article by Sir Bryan Fell written in August 1935: 'Nineteenth Century and After', Vol. CXVIII, pp. 129–41.

[53] Sir David resigned the Conservative Whip in January 1959. At the General Election of October 1959, he defeated a Labour opponent by 5,725 votes.

[54] Richards, p. 13.

[55] 'Honest political dissent' does not mean the right of 630 individual M.P.s to voice their differing opinions on all subjects. This 'fallacy of self-defeating

individualism' (Crick: *Reform of the Commons*, 1959, p. 3.) would destroy Parliament's effectiveness. Lord Attlee has pointed out that the conception of Parliament as an assembly of individuals all using their individual judgement on every particular subject is 'hopelessly impractical' (*Fabian Journal*, November 1958, p. 8). Nigel Nicolson similarly concedes that party organization is needed to make vague aspirations 'articulate and effective'. (Nicolson, p. 17.) The general recognition of the necessity of some party organization and discipline has been mentioned above.

[56] Crossman, p. 18.

[57] Acland, p. 171.

[58] Ross: *Parliamentary Representation*, p. 209. The author does not conceive of this type of extended remuneration as a 'pension', but as a means of allowing the former Member to re-establish himself, outside Westminster, without suffering financial hardship.

[59] H.C. 72 of 1953/4.

[60] H.C. 72 of 1953/4, para 36.

[61] *The Times*, 8th March 1954, p. 9. The article agreed that an extended Members' Fund might be considered, but no general statutory right should exist.

[62] H.C. Deb. 613, c. 1183. Lady Tweedsmuir was speaking during the Second Reading of Mr. Speaker Morrison's Retirement Bill, on 18th November 1959.

[63] The question is discussed more fully in Chapter VI.

[64] Richards, p. 242. An excellent summary of the position regarding Members' pensions is given in the following pages of Richard's book, pp. 242–7.

[65] *The Times*, 17th February 1954, p. 9.

[66] *ibid.* 18th February 1954, p. 9. The related question of Members' pay is discussed in Chapter VII.

[67] In *The New Liberal Democracy*, Part II, p. 7.

[68] *op. cit.* 23–5. Foot adds, however, that more free votes will not be possible until the status of private Party meetings is diminished.

[69] Mr. Herbert (now Lord) Morrison, who is not a keen advocate of too many free votes, nevertheless declares that a Government should abide by the result when such a liberty has been granted (Morrison, p. 355).

[70] 'Democracy and Dictatorship' in *Political Quarterly*, Vol. IV, 1933, pp. 467–81.

[71] H.C. Deb. 399, cs. 1866–67.

[72] The relations between Parliament and the Executive are discussed in the following chapter.

[73] Bulmer-Thomas, p. 272.

[74] *Speeches and Letters on American Affairs*, Everyman edition, pp. 72–3. For an excellent summary of opinions in this matter, see Richards, pp. 157–72.

[75] At the Selwyn Hall, Boscombe, 5th December 1956.

[76] Nicolson, p. 166.

[77] *ibid.* p. 167.

[78] Morrison says of Nicolson's *People and Parliament*: 'In general I agree with the views he expressed in it.' (Morrison, p.353.) A leading article in *The Times* of 3rd October 1958 similarly approved of the author's general principles, (p. 11). Following a postal ballot in February 1959 among members of his constituency association, Nigel Nicolson was defeated (by 91 votes) and did not stand at the 1959 General Election.

[79] Chapter I: 'Elections and Representation'.

[80] See also note 55, above.

81 cf. a diagram in *Our Parliament*, p. 167: 'The Struggle for Time—II, The Precious Initiative of the Private Member.'
82 *ibid*. p. 167.
83 H.C. Deb. 615, cs. 1456ff.
84 S.O. No. 4.
85 A pre-war Wednesday sitting is, very approximately, about half as long again as a post-war Friday sitting.
86 *An Introduction to the Procedure of the House of Commons*, 3rd ed., 1958, p. 114.
87 H.L. Deb. 183, c. 951. (The subject under discussion was the Protection of Wild Birds, 28th July 1953.)
88 Lord Winterton: H.C. Deb. 460, c. 80.
89 Ede: H.C. Deb. 507, c. 149.
90 H.C. 92 of 1958/9, Qs. 119, 995–6, p. 194.
91 H.C. 189 of 1945/6, para. 51.
92 *ibid*. para 29.
93 H.C. 92 of 1958/9, p. 11; and Qs. 802, 969.
94 H.C. 189 of 1945/6.
95 *ibid*.
96 *Speed up Law Reform*, pp. 27–8.
97 H.C. 129 of 1931/2, p. xvii.
98 Muir, p. 205.
99 Stewart, p. 118.
100 Bromhead: *Private Members' Bills*, pp. 42–3.
101 *Speed up Law Reform*, pp. 27–8.
102 Cited by Pollard, *op. cit*. p. 29.
103 *ibid*. p. 28.
104 Under this procedure, Acts can be consolidated, and have minor improvements made in them, by a Joint Committee; subsequent progress of the Consolidated Bill in both Houses is largely formal.
105 *Speed up Law Reform*, p. 27.
106 H.C. 92 of 1958/9, paras. 15–16.
107 *Political Quarterly*, Vol. XXVIII, 1957, pp. 32–9.
108 *Speed up Law Reform*, p. 29.
109 Gordon, p. 167.
110 See section (*a*) above.
111 This very sensible distinction between *power* and *influence* is made by Richards in *op. cit*. p. 260.
112 Hollis in *The Establishment: A Symposium*, p. 175.
113 *Listener*, 26th January 1956, pp. 127–8.
114 King-Hall, H.C. Deb. 400, 26th May 1944, cs. 1087–8. H. Eckstein: *Pressure Group Politics: The Case of the British Medical Association*, 1960; S. E. Finer: *Anonymous Empire*, 1958; J. D. Stewart: *British Pressure Groups: Their Role in Relation to the House of Commons*, 1958. There have also been numerous articles on the subject.
115 Lord Campion and others, p. 26.
116 In *The Unservile State*, Book I, Chap. 2, pp. 27ff.
117 H.C. Deb. 612, c. 217. (Business of the House: Private Members' Time; 28th October 1959. The speaker was Nigel Fisher.)

V

Parliament and the Executive

(*a*) CABINET AND PARLIAMENT

An outstanding constitutional development of the first half of the present century has been the substantial increase of the Cabinet's authority and activities. To a large extent this development was prompted by the advent of two world wars within a relatively short space; but the enhanced powers of the Cabinet (and, consequently, of the Executive as a whole) survived into the post-war years, and the relationship between Parliament and the Executive has become a major peace-time issue. Our modern system of democracy has been termed 'Parliamentary bureaucracy',[1] 'Cabinet Government',[2] and 'Cabinet bureaucracy';[3] whether such definitions emphasize the superiority of the Executive or of the House of Commons, it is clear that no account of proposed reforms for the latter would be complete without considering the mutual interdependence of these two great bodies.

Apart from extremist views such as those of Mosley and his present or former supporters,[4] recent opinion has accepted unanimously the need for both these aspects of the constitution. The difficulty is the preservation (some would say, 'the discovery') of a fair, effective balance between the Parliamentary and bureaucratic elements—for an unhappy marriage between the two could develop into a most dangerous situation for the nation. And from the briefest survey of relevant criticisms, it is beyond doubt that most writers regard the unprecedented authority of Cabinet and Executive as the true source of existing dissatisfaction. The Cabinet is too omnipotent, declared Muir in 1930; by subjecting Parliament to its power, it has 'atrophied' control on behalf of the nation by the latter's elected representatives.[5] In the House of

For Notes and References see pages 139–142

Lords on 17th May 1950, Lord Cecil of Chelwood moved to resolve 'that the growing power of the Cabinet is a danger to the democratic constitution of the country', and countless others have found it difficult to reconcile such 'growing power' with democracy. In his *Reform of the Commons*, Bernard Crick claims that 'the Executive has reached a point where the divorce in attitude between Minister and M.P. is such that both front-benches have grown more and more prone to think that Parliamentary criticism is nuisance enough at the moment, without contemplating radical reforms of Parliamentary procedure.'[6] Edward F. Iwi, recalling how Parliament has in the past defended its powers successfully against the Monarch, adds that it is now delegating its authority, almost recklessly, to the Executive, which is now the strongest component in our Constitution.[7] Because of his professionally unbiased position, one can do no better than quote again as representative the view of the late Lord Campion, who regretted the increasing subordination of the Commons to the Executive, through the influence of Ministers.[8]

Here we find the main theme of the present chapter. How can we arrive at the best possible compromise between liberty and authority—between Parliament and Government—which Lord Salisbury described as 'the basis of ordered freedom'?[9] The problem is difficult and delicate, but not insuperable: there is, as Crick points out, no necessary contradiction between desiring both a strong Executive and a strong, efficient Commons.[10] The question is too complex, however, to be dealt with in a single, tidy chapter; related matters such as the influence of the Party system, the question of Private Members' time in the House, and proposals for an extended system of Committees are discussed more fully elsewhere. Moreover, the internal workings of the Civil Service proper are not considered here, unless directly involved in some specific suggestion for parliamentary reform. The present chapter is thus concerned primarily with the structure and responsibilities of the Cabinet, regarded as the link between Parliament and the Executive; with the Cabinet's influence on the duties and effectiveness of the ordinary Member of Parliament; and with the questions of Parliament's control over delegated legislation and nationalized industries.

(b) THE OFFICE OF PRIME MINISTER[11]

The whole *modus operandi* of the Cabinet depends very largely on the ability and personality of the Prime Minister, whose position, once elected, is one of great authority. Suggesting that the best name for our constitution is 'elective monarchy', R. W. K. Hinton has explained: 'Government by a single person is monarchy, and it is because the Prime Minister is the real ruler that I think our constitution ought to be called a monarchy. We recognise this practice when we vote.'[12] As Laski has remarked, little short of carefully organized revolt can shake his position within or without the Cabinet, and the Professor goes on to point out that a problem of real constitutional significance is involved in this growth of the Prime Minister's powers: 'Great authority may . . . . accrue to one, the greatness of whose leadership may fairly be regarded as doubtful'.[13] That Laski is thinking in particular of Neville Chamberlain is quite clear from what follows; his fears are that the mistakes of an authoritative Premier may leave Parliament, and even the Cabinet, with nothing better than a chance of *ex post facto* control which (as in the Munich crisis) could come too late.[14] The seriousness of the whole question of the power of the Prime Minister in Parliament is heightened, in the view of many, by the method of his appointment: 'It is still the Monarch who selects the individual who is likely to make the most effective Prime Minister, and that individual who acts on his own responsible judgement of the situation.'[15] Thus the two institutions of Government (the Prime Minister and the Cabinet he selects) and of Parliament are to some extent at least separate, independent entities—each starting from separate historical origins and each perpetuating itself by its own methods.[16] Since the Cabinet remains in essence a 'Committee of the party in power', one may fairly say that this question of the Prime Minister's appointment attracts serious criticism only when that same party has no obvious leader to assume the mantle of supreme authority. An example occurred on the resignation of Sir Anthony Eden. Would his successor be Mr. Harold Macmillan or Mr. R. A. Butler? Speculation was widespread, but the responsibility of making the final choice rested not with the people or Parliament, or even with the Conservative Party, but with the Queen. The exercise of the royal prerogative at this juncture aroused much comment—was it asking too much of Her Majesty, at a comparatively young age, to select a Prime Minister who would then choose his own Cabinet?[17] There is the added risk that on such occasions the Sovereign may become involved in party politics.[18]

The problem, as summarized above, is twofold: is it desirable to limit the Prime Minister's authority, and is his method of appointment sufficiently democratic? To begin with the latter question, one may say that there have been more criticisms than constructive proposals for reform.[19] Referring to the Australian system of choice by the party caucus, Laski observes that such a method does not always make for that mutual confidence between a Premier and his back-benchers which the British system does.[20] Laski means that the Sovereign normally chooses the man which the party in power has itself singled out as its leader. But since this leader is not always an obvious choice (as has been seen above), the Professor's defence of the British method of appointment is not totally waterproof. He also mentions 'the French system of continuous, though short-lived, coalitions in which each group insists to the Prime Minister both upon his choice of certain men, and, hardly less, of the places they must occupy . . . .'[21] and concludes 'that that profoundly highly influences the tendency of a French Cabinet to move towards dissolution upon the day the Chamber has given to it its first vote of confidence'.[22] In 1957, the Labour Party outlined the procedure it wished to see adopted if a Labour Premier were to be appointed under similar conditions. It declared that the Monarch should not make the appointment until a new leader had been elected by the Parliamentary Labour Party. This meant that there would be no question of leaving the real choice in the hands of the Monarch.[23] No wholly acceptable alternative to the present method of choosing the Prime Minister has been discovered to date, however. Those who point out its dangers, yet favour its retention, rely on the ultimate safeguards of public opinion and the need for party unity as means of ousting a man whose appointment proves to be a mistake.

As to possible limitations on a Prime Minister's powers, once elected, Laski has two suggestions for reform, and both underline the need for *collective* Cabinet responsibility. Firstly, no Prime Minister should submit to the Sovereign a request for dissolution until he has obtained full Cabinet assent. In a deeply divided Cabinet, the personal power of one man to seek a dissolution might stifle honest dissent, force the resignations of able Ministers, or promote intrigue and confusion in the whole Government.[24] This personal power of asking for a dissolution is also emphasized by Carter, who points out that the American President has obviously no comparable power of dissolution over Congress.[25] Laski also disapproves of the limits a Prime Minister may set to the circulation of Cabinet papers; if the Cabinet is to remain a 'unit' then no Minister should be held responsible for an action of which he has not been fully and opportunely informed.[26]

Such reforms are not the whole answer to the problem; Laski himself, who saw the increasing authority of the Prime Minister as one aspect of the process of centralization taking place in all spheres of government, admits that.[27] He adds that the most effective reform to limit such powers is likely to occur in the area of the Premier's relations with his party, both inside and outside the House of Commons, and that a national crisis might well precipitate a constitutional change of this sort.[28] There remains, however, one indirect means of limiting or modifying the Prime Minister's position—reform of the Cabinet structure as a whole.

(c) THE CABINET

As has been seen, there is no inherent contradiction between a desire for a vigilant, efficient House of Commons on the one hand, and a desire for a strong, policy-making team of Ministers on the other. Hence, suggested reforms deal not only with Parliament's control over the Executive, but also with the welfare and effectiveness of the Government's representatives. Amery, amongst many others, has asserted that the present Cabinet machinery is totally inadequate for the immensely wide, complex responsibilities now facing Ministers.[29] His principal contention is that a group of overworked departmental chiefs, absorbed in the details of their respective routines, is not a fit body to plan vital long-term policy and see that it is properly carried out. When each Minister attempts to 'father' the wishes of his own Department, the Cabinet is inevitably subject to internal friction and delay, and is unable to make collective decisions on important, supra-departmental matters.[30] Amery's suggested remedy, illustrated in the diagram below, is that a definite division should be made, within the Government, between policy and administration.[31]

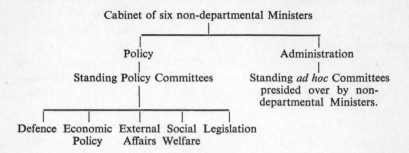

Cabinet of six non-departmental Ministers

Policy — Administration

Standing Policy Committees — Standing *ad hoc* Committees presided over by non-departmental Ministers.

Defence Economic External Social Legislation
Policy Affairs Welfare

A smaller Cabinet, as above, with its subordinate committee-system, would then be able to perform the vital work of supervision and co-ordination. A similar suggestion for a small inner Cabinet of non-departmental Ministers engaged essentially in the formation of policy was made in an unsigned article in *The Economist* on 27th October 1934,[32] and since Amery published his views, they have received considerable support.[33]

Others have pointed out the potential defects of such proposals. Firstly, the creation of a small, formal ministerial hierarchy could easily promote jealousies and frustration within and without the Cabinet.[34] Laski, whilst agreeing that the traditional Cabinet is too large,[35] could not believe that the separation between policy and administration would be as easy as Amery suggests.[36] The latter, Laski adds, was probably influenced by an unduly roseate view of Lloyd George's Cabinet in 1916–19: what is best in times of war is not always most suitable for peace.[37] A more serious objection to Amery's proposals is that a 'Policy Minister' might not be able to control a 'subordinate' Minister having all the status and executive power of his Department behind him.[38] Moreover, to conceive of 'policy meetings' in the absence of departmental chiefs is unrealistic; discussion of general principles must involve consideration of detail, and Amery's Cabinet would not have such details at its finger-tips.[39] Finally, would a select group of backroom boys brooding over future policy be able to afford effective, informed political leadership to the Party in power, to the House of Commons, and to the country as a whole? Lord Morrison does not believe it could.[40] He observes that Amery, in his enthusiasm, has carried his idea too far, and adds that it is possible both to avoid the very large Cabinet[41] and to use non-departmental Ministers to secure a measure of co-ordination and policy planning without restricting the Cabinet to six super-Ministers.

In the Romanes Lecture of 1946, Sir John Anderson (later Lord Waverley) also brought forward the criticism that supervising Ministers without portfolio were not a practical proposition, since their existence would clash with the accepted parliamentary responsibilities of departmental chiefs.[42] Instead, Sir John suggested a careful development of the system of Cabinet Committees; there would be groups to consider Defence, Economic Policy, Foreign Relations, Social Welfare, Establishment Affairs and Legislation, special attention being given to general policy. Joint meetings between two or more of these groups would contribute to co-ordination of policy. A similar suggestion was made by a committee of Conservatives in the same year, in a publication called 'Some Proposals for Constitutional Reform'. For Economic Policy, for instance, the Chancellor of the Exchequer should preside over a Standing Committee of Ministers, which would supervise economic research, report regularly to the Cabinet on trade, agriculture, etc., and also to Parliament. Sub-Committees would exist for particular economic problems, and Civil Servants, as well as outside representatives of industry, would participate in these.[43] These suggestions aim at extending and elaborating, rather than at innovating: since, to a certain extent, the system of Cabinet Committees has been realized already. Lord Morrison has given a first-hand account of their functioning under the Labour Government of 1945–50.[44] He concludes that they saved the Cabinet a great amount of work, without impairing the doctrine of ultimate collective Cabinet responsibility. With a few exceptions,[45] the existence of these Committees was kept secret during the Labour Government's period of office—a policy which Anderson himself had advocated.

Agreeing with Anderson's contention that supervising Ministers are not a practical proposition, Lord Morrison has elaborated his objections with particular reference to Winston Churchill's so-called 'Overlord' system. In October 1951, the appointment was announced of Lord Leathers as Secretary of State for the Coordination of Transport, Fuel and Power; simultaneously, Lord Woolton was given supervisory authority over the Ministers of Agriculture and Food. Attlee criticized these appointments on several grounds. Above all, he raised the important constitutional issue of answerability to the House of Commons: 'Here it seems that the power of decision is left with Ministers in another place, and we here are to be faced only with departmental Ministers responsible merely for administration. I want to know this: when questions of major policy arise concerning food and agriculture and transport and fuel and power, who will answer in this House?'[46] Morrison added his objections to those of Attlee. The House faced a position, he declared, in which Ministers not in the Commons had been given public and specific responsibilities which could not but move certain responsibilities away from the departmental Ministers concerned. There could be no fair comparison between these 'Overlords' and the system of Cabinet Committees used by the Labour Government—these latter (secret) Committees were the domestic concern of the party in power, and there was no question of the Chairman of such Committees being answerable to the Commons.[47] The 'Overlord' system eventually came to an end in September 1953, with the resignation of Lord Leathers. There had been sharp disagreement between supporters and opponents of the idea, and it must be admitted that neither side was able to convince the other as to its notion of the precise responsibilities of the 'Overlords'.

Morrison has drawn the important distinction between a 'supervising' and a 'co-ordinating' Minister. Whereas his feeling is that the former imperils an essential of the constitution—namely, a departmental Minister's accountability to Parliament—he does concede that the volume and complexity of Cabinet business make out a strong case for a sprinkling of senior 'co-ordinating' Ministers. The latter normally work as Chairmen of Cabinet Committees; they can advise, consult, urge and persuade; they can view the policy of a single Department against the broader background of the several other Departments which they seek to co-ordinate. But a co-ordinator 'is a helpful colleague and not a master'—there is no question of his impairing the responsibility to Parliament of the individual political heads of Departments.[48] The idea of co-ordination within the Cabinet is not new. In 1937, Attlee had argued in favour of non-departmental appointments which would facilitate both Cabinet cohesion and policy-planning.[49] When he became Prime Minister, he sought to secure 'supervision without blurring the responsibility of departmental Ministers',[50] and two senior Ministers—Morrison and Greenwood—became Cabinet co-ordinators.[51]

A miscellany of other proposed Cabinet reforms may be mentioned briefly here. Advancing the familiar thesis that a Minister can attend either to his Cabinet papers or to his Department, but not to both, Desmond Donnelly has suggested that day-to-day control of the Departments should be vested in the Parliamentary Secretaries, who would also answer most Questions in the House. Ministers would deal with major departmental policies, but their principal concern would be the Cabinet.[52] Apart from relieving an overworked Minister, this scheme would clearly add to the status of the Parliamentary Secretary—which Ellen Wilkinson, in a profoundly melancholy moment, described as 'less than the dust'. Lord Mansfield proposed in July 1938 that Ministers should be able to address the House to which they did not belong. They could thus answer attacks made on them in 'another place'; good Ministers would never have to resign on receiving a peerage; it would be easier for the Premier himself to be a peer. Lord Crewe, however, felt that such an innovation would increase a Minister's burdens and reduce still further the status of Parliamentary Secretaries. An added complication would stem from the differences in practice and procedure between the two Houses. Lord Londonderry also listed practical obstacles in the way of this reform, whilst Lord Onslow felt that peers might not attend in the Lords if their hopes of office were diminished in this fashion.[53] The idea has nevertheless come to the fore again, in dramatic fashion, following the controversial appointment in July 1960 of a peer (Lord Home) to the office of Foreign Secretary. Then there is the suggestion that there should be a special Ministry of Research, the work of which would be divorced from the responsibilities of actual administrative routine. The Haldane Committee[54] favoured such a Ministry. But both Amery and Laski rejected this proposal, the latter in particular maintaining that research which is to affect policy must be controlled by those who are directing policy. Research undertaken in an academic fashion would not have that sense of reality vital to its success.[55] Laski similarly points out that proper contact between research and the realities of everyday political administration is absent from the idea of an Economic General Staff, of which Lord Beveridge was an enthusiastic advocate. As a practical illustration of this potential defect, Laski claims that much of the value of the 'Beveridge' Report on Social Insurance and Allied Services came from its principal author's previous practical experience as an official at the Ministry of Labour.[56] Finally, we have Philip Goodhart's antidote for front-bench fatigue: the ministerial sabbatical year. A number of Ministers and/or Parliamentary Secretaries should be 'rested' every year, and have the opportunity of refreshing mind and body —for further front-bench exertions on their return—in the Caribbean, Paris or Hampstead Garden Suburb. An innovation of this sort would also make it possible for the Premier to 'spread the chance of promotion and so reduce feelings of frustration below the gangway'.[57]

To sum up, it is clear that supporters of the scheme for a very small supervisory peace-time Cabinet of 'Policy Ministers' are outnumbered by their critics. The latter point out in particular that policy and departmental administration are in practice inseparable, and that the answerability to Parliament of heads of Departments might well be confused if there were 'super-Ministers' above them. But there is almost general agreement that present-day Cabinets tend to be too large. The authors of the 1918 'Machinery of Government' Report advocated a Cabinet membership of from ten to twelve.[58] Muir thought ten an ideal number for general efficiency and collective responsibility.[59] Laski set the limit at fifteen, the Secretary of State for Scotland and the Lord Chancellor being excluded under his scheme.[60] A Cabinet of 'moderate size, say sixteen to eighteen' seemed to Morrison to be the best solution.[61] There is also substantial support for a good measure of general policy-planning and 'co-ordination', to be effected by senior Ministers within the Cabinet and by the use of Cabinet Committees, rather than by 'Overlords'. One suspects that three major requirements, or aims, motivate the bulk of these proposals.

The first is to enhance the collective responsibility of the Cabinet on all important questions of policy, in order that such great decisions should not be made wholly on the initiative of the Prime Minister, or of a small caucus within the Cabinet itself. As Sir David Lindsay Keir puts it, genuine Cabinet solidarity ensures that the administrative business of the nation is co-ordinated by a unanimous collective will.[62] The second aim is intimately related to the first. Since the Cabinet is the link between a permanent Executive and Parliament, it is vital that Members should themselves know that the Cabinet is genuinely 'collectively responsible' for major items of policy. Only if this is so can effective control on behalf of the people become a reality. It is particularly important that the Cabinet should be regarded as a unit when a vote of confidence is taken—since each Cabinet Minister is staking his position, in theory at least, on the result.[63] The third, and most obvious, point of proposed Cabinet reorganization is the increased efficiency of the Cabinet itself. This last objective is not incompatible with the other two: as has been said already, there is no automatic contradiction between desiring both a strong, efficient Executive and a keen, effectively critical Parliament.

Up to now, the question of the relationship between Parliament and the Executive has been considered from the viewpoint of the Cabinet and its head, the Prime Minister. In addition, of course, there have been proposals aimed at effecting a better balance between Parliament and the Executive by increasing the powers of the ordinary M.P. over the Cabinet. The majority of these suggestions concern the opportunities afforded the private Member of raising grievances and of initiating legislation in the House: these are discussed in the chapters devoted to Procedure and to the Party System respectively. There remain to be considered here three outstanding problems. To what extent has the growth of delegated legislation impaired the prestige and effectiveness of Parliament? Should Parliament's control over nationalized undertakings be extended and/or tightened? And finally, is there a place in our constitutional set-up for a British 'Ombudsman'?

(d) DELEGATED LEGISLATION

A subject on which Parliament and the Executive can cross swords is Delegated Legislation—the granting by Parliament of certain areas of its legislative powers, with safeguards, to Ministers. The principle of delegated legislation is one that is attacked on two fronts; first, that Parliament's sovereignty over the legislative machine is gainsaid; secondly, that the setting-up of administrative tribunals can prove to be a derogation of the Rule of Law. This second principle carries us rather far from our subject of Parliamentary (as opposed to Law) Reform; but the first principle is in the heart of the subject. Lord Hewart's *The New Despotism* (1928) struck out at the abuses that had grown up; the Donoughmore Committee on Ministers' Powers was set up to consider them, and to report what safeguards were necessary to secure the principles of the sovereignty of Parliament and the supremacy of the law. Their report, says Sir Cecil Carr, was comforting.[64] 'The country was told that delegated legislation was valuable and indeed inevitable. The Committee suggested that, with reasonable vigilance and proper precautions, we had nothing to fear. . . .'

The Committee made a number of detailed recommendations, but two years later complaint was being made in the House that effect had not been given to them.[66] In 1937, although one member could say: 'The particular clauses against which [*The New Despotism*] was written . . . are finding their way less and less into modern statutes.'[67] Another said: 'I believe that almost every week in this House the Executive is usurping the function of Parliament.'[68] In 1944, it was still being said that it was time to enforce the Donoughmore proposals.[69]

Meanwhile, the problem has increased in size; in 1950, about three times as many Instruments of general—as opposed to local—applicability were made as pre-1931 (during the war, the number had reached nearly five times as many).[70]

Needless to say, this increased use of delegated powers has not lacked supporters. Ponsonby[71] and Dalton[72] in the thirties, Stewart in the fifties, for example, have all gone on record in thinking that more, and not less, legislation should be delegated. Acts of Parliament should, they say, state broad general principles; the details should be left to the Minister to work out.

But criticism has continued and in 1943 the House of Commons set up—in accordance with one of the Donoughmore Committee's recommendations—a Select Committee which scrutinizes every Instrument laid before the House on which the House may or must move a resolution. The Committee draws the attention of the House to any Instrument that appears to make unusual or unexpected use of the power conferred by the parent statute. Carr says of this Committee that '. . . it acts with independence and without partisanship; it can do so because it is debarred from reporting on matters of policy or merits; it is entirely uninfluenced by the Executive, and it has established the interesting convention that its chairman must be a member of the Opposition'. Its work, however, he says, is imperfectly geared to the machinery of parliamentary control; Members table their motions for annulling Instruments long before the Committee has reported on them, and the reasons for their challenge will probably be reasons which the Committee was debarred from considering.[73]

The setting-up of this Committee might have been a modest step forward, but various powerful indictments of the whole system continued to appear. The works of Sir Carleton Allen,[74] W. A. Robson,[75] G. W. Keeton (who was able to cite the case of Crichel Down)[76], and Carr,[77] among others, have framed the case. Curtis cites the following among their main criticisms:[78]

(i)   Delegated legislation is sometimes made on matters of principle, and may therefore result in an evasion of parliamentary statute.

(ii) Taxing power is occasionally delegated.

(iii) There has been some retrospective legislation.

(iv) Sub-delegation is always dangerous.

(v)   The courts of law are by-passed.

(vi) The legislation is not always well-publicized, so that it is possible to offend against it in ignorance.

(vii) Parliamentary control is unsatisfactory.

As far as this last complaint is concerned, various amelioratives have been put forward. Thus, Campion suggested to the Select Committee on Procedure in 1946 that the Statutory Instruments Committee should be empowered to report on the *merits* of Instruments, and to inquire into grievances out of those Instruments actually in operation.[79] The Committee agreed that this scheme 'would go some way to supplement the inadequate and unsatisfactory opportunities which the House . . . possesses for exercising . . . control', but considered it was beyond the scope of their investigation, and urged that a later Committee should be set up to consider the specific matter.[80]

Those who support the idea of 'departmental' Committees—Committees, that is, which will specialize in the work of a particular Ministry, and can act as a link between the House and the department—sometimes urge that these Committees will be able to supervise the delegated legislation which emanates from that department.[81] Pollard, for instance, suggested that, if the departmental Committees do not agree on the need for a particular Instrument, then it should be left to the House to affirm or reject it.[82] It is interesting in this context to note that the Select Committee on Procedure in 1957 recommended that, provided certain safeguards were allowed, debates on affirmative resolutions relating exclusively to Scotland should take place in the Scottish Standing Committee.[83]

A Select Committee was set up by the House of Commons in 1952 to cover all this field of delegated legislation; in so doing they resurrected and reconsidered those of the Donoughmore proposals which had not yet been brought into force. Principal among these was the suggestion that each House of Parliament should set up a sessional Committee to examine every bill for the purpose of drawing attention to any unusual or novel proposal in it to delegate legislative authority.[84] Such a Committee, was, said Carr, 'potentially more valuable' than the other Scrutiny Committee which had been set up;[85] but the Select Committee disagreed with the idea, preferring to rely on the vigilance of private members.[86]

Among the more important of the other questions which members of this Select Committee asked themselves, in seeking to improve the House's control over delegated legislation, were these:

(i) Should the Government issue with each bill a memorandum explaining what sort of powers are to be delegated by it?

130

(ii)   Should there be a Committee of the House to consider all S.I.s, and separate the important ones from the less important?

(iii) Should Statutory Instruments be amendable?

(iv)   Could the resolutions relating to Statutory Instruments be taken in a Committee, rather than in the House?

(v)   Should a Minister have to explain his proposals to a Committee before laying his Instruments?

(vi)   Should the House meet at special times—say, in the morning—to debate prayers for annulling S.I.s?

These questions span most of the proposals still current for the better controlling by Parliament of delegated legislation; the Committee, with great consistency, answered each one in the negative.[87]

One proposal they did make, and which the House adopted, was that debates on prayers to annul Instruments should be concluded at a definite hour. This prevented such debates from continuing indefinitely into the night, and made sure they would be conducted on the merits of the motion, rather than as a weapon of obstruction. But this was a change more of convenience than of principle.

The main charge remains. Committees of inquiry may continue to find that the sovereignty of Parliament over delegated legislation is secure; but if Parliament is content to divest itself of its powers, and give to the Executive the right to make Orders in Council under unlimited statutory powers, is not the trouble that Parliament is all too sovereign? This was the question that Carr, with his vast experience of the matter, posed.[88] He gave his own answer thus:

With the intensification of party politics, parliamentary control has . . . in effect disappeared; when . . . the Government side has secured the enactment of the parent statute, the Opposition side has little hope of success in moving a motion for the annulment of the resultant Statutory Instrument. These are issues of political partisanship, not of political theory. Only the Opposition will be challenging the Executive, and the Executive has the means and the will to crush the challenge.[89]

131

(e) PARLIAMENTARY CONTROL OVER NATIONALIZED INDUSTRIES

In the earliest of the nationalized undertakings—such as the Post Office, the Royal Ordnance factories, and the state management of public houses in Carlisle—responsibility and powers were vested wholly in the Minister for the Department involved. Accordingly he was answerable in Parliament for everything to do with those undertakings, and parliamentary control could be said to be total.

In the inter-war years, however, a new type of nationalized undertaking came into being—the public corporation; early examples were the B.B.C., the London Passenger Transport Board and the Central Electricity Board. In these cases, governmental control was indirect.

Much of the political argument on the subject in the thirties was directed to the point of whether subsequent undertakings should be controlled by a Minister or a Board; with the nationalization of the transport and power industries after 1945—and the acceptance of the public corporation as the type to be employed[90] —much of this argument becomes only of academic interest. To-day's problem is a post-war one.

The post-war nationalization Acts place a number of duties upon the Minister—and on these points, of course, the Minister is answerable to Parliament; these duties are noticeably more extensive than those of Ministers in respect of the pre-war Corporations.[91] The pattern of these Acts is to give the Minister the responsibility for nominating members of the Board; the power of issuing general directions to the Board on matters affecting the national interest; and certain wide controls over the Board's finances.[92] To this extent, parliamentary control could be openly exercised; but beyond it, as one of the chief architects of nationalization pointed out, '. . . the precise character of the public accountability of these Boards [had] to be worked out in the light of experience'.[93]

This 'working out' has occasioned much thinking, both inside and outside Parliament. In 1950, Morrison listed six ways in which the House of Commons could exercise control over the Boards;[94] but his list was, said Goodhart, 'more formidable in length than in content',[95] and the House appeared to believe that, as things were, it was not able to exercise effective control.

The first battle that the House had to fight was over its right to ask Parliamentary Questions. If the Minister has no direct responsibility for a matter, he cannot be questioned on the point: and thus many Questions on nationalized industries had to be refused by the Table. The Speaker, however, allowed a relaxation of the rules to be made. Questions on nationalized industries which he deemed to be of sufficient public importance would in future be allowed. The Minister could still, theoretically, refuse to answer the Question, but the right of asking it was formally admitted.[96]

While this might have been a palliative, it was hardly a cure for the House's complaint. The next step was to set up a Select Committee to enquire into the relationship between the House and the industries, and this occurred in 1951. Its first report dealt with Questions and it concurred in the view that 'Questions on matters of detail in the Nationalized Industries are inappropriate'.[97] This point is of particular significance for, as a paper published by the Acton Society Trust has pointed out, Members, both in Questions they attempt to ask and the speeches they make, are preoccupied with local problems of management as opposed to overall efficiency.[98]

It should be added, on the subject of Questions, that the Boards make special provision for the answering of the letters sent to them by individual members. The Chairman of one Board told the Select Committee that his average correspondence with Members was about 1,700 letters a year;[99] Morrison suggested that these letters gave 'fuller and perhaps more satisfactory information than could be condensed into a parliamentary answer'.[100] In his view (writing in 1954), the controversy about the eligibility of Parliamentary Questions had tended to diminish.[101] But with the decision of the House in 1958 that letters from M.P.s, forwarded to the Boards by the Minister, had only a qualified privilege, there were renewed demands for wider facilities for asking parliamentary questions.[102] In 1960, the Leader of the House promised that Ministers would in general view more broadly their responsibility for answering questions on the nationalized industries. *The Times* thought this indicated that some sensible progress was being made.[103]

In 1950 it was still being suggested that the Minister's control over the industries should become closer, thereby allowing Parliament the right of asking a greater area of Questions. Thus, Austen Albu said he thought the Minister himself should actually be Chairman of the Boards which he appoints.[104] But argument tended then to move on to different ground. If these Boards were not to be departmentally controlled, what other form of parliamentary control should be tried? Curtis suggests there were two possibilities open.[105] First, a Committee of Inquiry could be set up—perhaps on the lines of a Royal Commission—periodically; or secondly, the House could set up a Select Committee to act as some sort of link. The former idea was urged by Morrison.[106] The inquiries—he suggested they should take place every seven years—would be on the lines of those held into the affairs of the B.B.C. before its Charter is renewed every ten years. But, in the same debate, the alternative—of setting up a Select Committee of the House—was urged by Hugh Molson, now Lord Molson,[107] and supported by Members from both sides of the House. Molson's idea was that the Committee should report to the House from time to time, and that the House's annual debates on the nationalized industries should be founded on those reports.

The Select Committee which the House set up in 1951 to advise it on its future relationship towards the industries decided, in their Second Report, that there was a case for a permanent Select Committee to act along the lines that Molson had suggested.[108] The Committee should, it thought, have the help of an officer of the calibre of the Comptroller and Auditor-General, at least one accountant, and any other specialized staff it found necessary.

When this Committee was duly set up in 1955, however, it was not given the use of any special staff, and its terms of reference were restricted to exclude matters of ministerial policy, as well as matters of day-to-day administration within the industry.[109] These terms of reference, however, the Committee found altogether too restrictive, and they were able to make no progress.[110] Accordingly, when a new Committee was set up in 1956, its field of activity was left very general. However, by a piece of typical House of Commons practice, the Committee were given to understand that, while the former restrictions were not specified, the House hoped the Committee would keep off those subjects; and it was no surprise when the Committee, in one of their first reports, said: 'We have tried not to become involved as critics with the day-to-day administration of the Board on the one hand, and with matters of Government policy on the other.'[111]

The setting up of a Select Committee was accompanied by a number of gloomy forebodings. *The Times*, seeing the Committee as the creature of Parliament's distrust of the nationalized undertakings, thought that, under the new arrangement, long-range vigilance and wise forbearance would both wither.[112] The *Observer* 'could not see how (the Committee's) existence would appreciably alter the relations between Parliament and the Boards'.[113]

A vigorous critic of nationalization, R. Kelf-Cohen,[114] questioned the whole principle that the industries, as statutory bodies, could be accountable to Parliament at all. He quoted a former head of the B.B.C., Lord Reith, as saying that the Select Committee might end by controlling the industry. The plain simple fact is that Parliament could not cope with the problem unless the industries were converted into Departments of State; and if that happened, parliamentary business would be hopelessly overloaded.

However, the first Reports of the Select Committee brought about a change of heart, *The Times*, to some extent, retracting its earlier prognostications.[115] Kelf-Cohen, on the evidence of one Report for the Committee, said it was too early to judge the value of their work. They could only justify their existence if they provided a body of informal opinions in the House; to do so, they would have to work very hard. In their debates on the Reports, the House itself appeared to welcome them;[116] whilst one Member has suggested that there is need of two Select Committees on the Nationalized Industries—one dealing with transport, and the other with fuel and power.[117] However, it is still too early to say if the Select Committee is going to prove to make the difference which its supporters claim it will, or indeed if it has come to stay.

A general criticism of a Committee of this kind is that its members are 'amateurs, and experience has shown that a Parliamentary Committee cannot readily find out much more about a complex enterprise than its managers want to reveal'.[118] The Committee, it will be remembered, does not have the use of the technical staff which was recommended for it. That it may have been in need of such a staff can be implied from one of its Reports, where it says: 'In much of the enquiry, it was a case of laymen hearing technical evidence from one quarter only. Your Committee have been conscious of the absence of a yardstick by which to judge the performance of the Board.'[119]

In a Special Report,[120] the Committee considered the various kinds of specialized assistance which might make their work more effective. They had in mind no change in their general method of working, and they insisted that any special staff should be servants of Parliament, and not of the Executive. They recognized, furthermore, that they were on the edge of suggesting an innovation in the traditional way in which Select Committees have worked. After setting out the pros and cons of a number of different proposals, they left it to the House to decide whether the staff of the House should be augmented to include someone to offer them technical advice, or whether they should be allowed to call in an 'assessor', an expert adviser who would act in a special intimacy with the Committee.

The trumpet had given an uncertain sound; the House had no clear indication of what to do. The Special Report was not debated. After an interval, the Committee was set up again in the new Parliament, with the same terms of reference, and without the mention of any special assistance. An article in *The Times*,[121] however, noted that the new Committee was being assisted by two Clerks, and not one, as hitherto.

A different proposal for breaking through the technical barrier and assessing the efficiency of a nationalized industry had been posited by Morrison. He had been impressed by the work done by good industrial consultants, and suggested that the Boards should collectively create an industrial efficiency unit of their own, which would be available to investigate the troubles of any of them; it would report to the Board concerned. This idea which he put forward, when in office, to the nationalized Boards, did not meet with their approval. It was, they thought, a reflection on their ability and efficiency, and the idea was dropped.[122] Goodhart pointed out a deficiency in the idea—it did not make clear whether or not the recommendations of the unit should be binding on the Boards.[123] Advice might be valuable, but it was no substitute for dynamic and efficient management.

After making a detailed study of the Reports and Accounts

which the nationalized industries are statutorily required to lay before Parliament, Raymond Nottage has suggested that the Select Committee on Nationalized Industries should see that a code of conventions is laid down, which would make for brevity and effectiveness in those Reports. This could lead to a greatly improved relationship between Parliament and the industries.[124]

This problem of the accountability of the nationalized industries, perhaps more than any other discussed here, is still very much in flux; much of the writing on the subject has already been overtaken by events. Thus, Kelf-Cohen (writing in 1958) said that the persuasive and far-reaching influence of Ministers, acting outside their statutory powers, on the decision of the Board, was something Parliament hardly seemed to have noticed;[125] however, this is a subject of which, as a result of the reports of the Select Committee, Parliament is now very much aware. There is nevertheless essentially a paradox at the heart of the matter; how can you have a business free to fight its competitors in the commercial world, yet expected to behave as a public service under the control of a Minister answerable to Parliament? There is a chasm of difference between the politician saying 'We are trying to get the best of both worlds',[126] and the Coal Board's former Chairman referring to 'this kind of half world in which we live'.[127]

Recent proposals for a closer watch over the expenditure on nationalized industries have been mentioned above.[128] The emphatic way in which these proposals were put forward might seem to show that 'nationalization' is still sometimes treated very much as a political issue in the House.

Some progress is being made. It would have been unthinkable, during the nationalization debates of 1946/50, to suggest that ten years later a Select Committee would be able to publish reports, objectively assessing the performance of nationalized Boards, and showing precious few differences of opinion between the stoutest propounders of each party's views. It might be that we are approaching the time when a suggestion such as Morrison's efficiency unit could be considered, without its being taken automatically to be a reflection on the Board's ability. So far, the Select Committee has conceived its function to be 'to acquaint the House with the activities and problems of the nationalized industries, to question those industries on the matters about which Members are most perplexed, and to report to the House with such comments as are appropriate'.[129] The House would then be sufficiently well-informed to take objective decisions. But if it is true, as Goodhart says,[130] that 'it is more in the threat of what it may do than in what it actually does, that the force of Parliamentary control lies', it may be that in the existence of a Select Committee with wide general terms of reference, capable of summoning before it any of the Boards' members which it thinks fit, capable of sending for any information it requires, the House has now got the instrument it needs.

(f) A BRITISH OMBUDSMAN?

Although there was a Justitieombudsman in Sweden as early as 1809, the Ombudsman who has recently attracted considerable attention is Professor Stephan Hurwitz of Denmark. The latter's office was created in 1953 under Section 55 of his country's new constitution, and Professor Hurwitz has himself written an account of his duties which aroused some interest in this country.[131] He further visited Britain in the spring of 1960, and broadcast on the subject. Donald McI. Johnson, an M.P. who has pleaded eloquently for a British Ombudsman, describes the Professor's functions thus: 'A Sir Andrew Clark in permanent session, inquiring and extracting papers, and commenting publicly upon the defects in the whole range of public administration—surprisingly, this is not far from what is happening in Denmark.'[132] The Ombudsman is not a Member of the Folketing—the essential point of his existence being that he is an impartial observer, or investigator, on behalf of the legislature. The need for such an independent, high-ranking official in Britain, with constitutional powers surpassing the dreams of the most zealous People's Leaguer, has been particularly emphasized since the John Waters case. To examine the facts of the 'Thurso Boy' case, a Tribunal had to be set up at very considerable cost. An Ombudsman would deal with such cases as part of his normal duties, and he would be able to deliver an authoritative, unbiased verdict as between the complainant and the administration. The prospects of Britain's acquiring an Ombudsman are, at present, uncertain. Supporters of the idea,[133] however, argue that such a person would go some way

towards restoring the balance between Parliament and Executive—
a vital need in the opinion of many whose criticisms and constructive proposals have been discussed in the present chapter.[134]

NOTES AND REFERENCES

[1] K. C. Wheare: 'The Machinery of Government' in *Public Administration*,
Vol. XXIV, pp. 75–85 (Inaugural lecture at Oxford, 16th November 1945).

[2] Jennings: *Cabinet Government*, 3rd ed., 1959.

[3] Lord Salter in *Parliament: A Survey*, Chap. V.

[4] See, for example, an article by Strachey and Joad: 'Parliamentary Reform:
The New Party's Proposals', in *Political Quarterly*, Vol. II, 1931, pp. 319–36.
Parliament's role is here virtually restricted to that of placing in office a
Government with full powers to govern.

[5] Muir discusses the 'ineffective' control of the Executive by Parliament at
length (pp. 41–80), as well as the 'dictatorship' of the Cabinet (pp. 87–106).

[6] Fabian Tract 319; p. 2.

[7] Iwi: *Laws and Flaws: Lapses of the Legislators*, 1956, p. 107.

[8] Lord Campion and others, pp. 25–6.

[9] H.L. Deb. 167, c. 360.

[10] Crick: *Reform of the Commons*, 1959, p. 2. Wedgwood Benn made the
same point in a recent Commons debate on Accommodation: H.C. Deb.,
31st March 1960.

[11] Professor Byrum E. Carter's book of that name was first published in
1956. It is a long account of the subject, both from the historical and the
practical points of view. Wiseman, however, rightly observes that Carter's
work contains certain errors and misleading generalizations (*Parliamentary
Affairs*, Vol. XII, No. 2, 1959, p. 243).

[12] Broadcast on the Third Programme, 6th January 1960, and published in
Parliamentary Affairs, Vol. XIII, No. 3, 1960, pp. 297–303.

Tom Clarke, in *My Northcliffe Diary*, 1931, p. 108, tells an anecdote which,
whilst clearly exaggerated and not to be taken too seriously, brings out the
extent to which this personal influence can be carried: 'The other day in Red
Wharf Bay, Anglesey, I was looked upon as a heathen by a Welsh newsagent
when I asked for the *Daily Mail*. . . . "Nobody in these parts reads that lying
rag, look you," said the man, "except a silly old man in Pentraeth, indeed.
Stick you to the *Daily News* and Lloyd George". He went on to protest so
much about the virtues of Lloyd George that I interposed, "But he's not God,
you know". "Ah, indeed, no, you are right", was the reply," but he is young
yet, look you!" '

Winston Churchill himself said: 'In any sphere of action there can be no
comparison between the positions of number one and number two, three, or
four. The duties and the problems of all persons other than number one are
quite different and in many ways more difficult. It is always a misfortune when
number two or three has to initiate a dominant plan or policy.' (Cited by
Carter, pp. 331–32.)

[13] Laski, pp. 116–17.

[14] *ibid*, p. 119.

[15] Amery, pp. 27–8.

[16] *ibid*. p. 28.

[17] cf. *Manchester Guardian*, 11th and 12th January 1957. A similar problem faced King George V in 1923 when Bonar Law retired: see Iwi, pp. 107–9. It is of course well known that the Queen sought the advice of Sir Winston Churchill and Lord Salisbury in 1957, but the ultimate decision lay none the less with the monarch.

[18] Curtis, p. 69.

[19] For a factual summary, see Carter, pp. 42ff.

[20] Laski, p. 112.

[21] *ibid*. p. 112. (Laski gave this lecture in 1950, i.e. before General de Gaulle became first President of the new Republic.)

[22] *ibid*., pp. 112–13.

[23] Marshall & Moodie: *Some Problems of the Constitution*, 1959, p. 62.

[24] Laski, pp. 113–14.

[25] Carter, pp. 335–6.

[26] Laski, p. 115.

[27] *ibid*. p. 119.

[28] *ibid*. pp. 119–20.

[29] Amery, p. 86. In his proposed remedies for these defects (see the following pages) Amery was much influenced by Lloyd George's 'War Cabinet', composed at the outset of five members.

[30] *ibid*. pp. 86–7.

[31] Taken from Curtis, p. 77.

[32] Vol. CXIX, pp. 765–6.

[33] e.g. Hollis: *Can Parliament Survive?*, p. 94; and Lord Samuel, who thought many administrative mistakes had been made because Ministers had so little opportunity for thinking ahead (H.L. Deb. 171, cs. 1087–89). He favoured a 'policy Cabinet' of 10–12 Ministers.

[34] Curtis, p. 77.

[35] Laski, p. 126.

[36] *ibid*. p. 130.

[37] *ibid*. p. 131. The same point was made in the 1918 'Machinery of Government' Report: Cd. 9230, p. 5.

[38] *ibid*, p. 132; Carter, p. 340; Morrison, pp. 52–3.

[39] Laski, p. 134: Carter, p. 340.

[40] Morrison, pp. 34–5.

[41] That is, a Cabinet of about 23 Members such as Mr. Neville Chamberlain's Cabinet in the spring of 1939.

[42] Published by O.U.P., 1946.

[43] *op. cit*. p. 126. The committee which made these proposals included Lord Ridley, Lady Davidson, and Mr. K. W. M. (now Sir Kenneth) Pickthorn.

[44] Morrison, pp. 16–27.

[45] No secret was made, for example, of the existence of the Defence Committee, under the chairmanship of the Prime Minister, since it was the successor of the Committee of Imperial Defence.

[46] H.C. Deb. 493, cs. 66–7.

[47] These arguments are discussed at some length in Morrison, pp. 45–54.

[48] These views are set out in detail in Morrison, pp. 53–5.

[49] In *The Labour Party in Perspective*, 1949.

[50] *As it Happened*, 1954, p. 152.

[51] *ibid*. p. 153.

[52] In a letter to *The Times*, 14th December 1956, p. 11.

[53] H.L. Deb. 110, cs. 579–611.

[54] Cd. 9230 (1918), p. 6, para. 14.
[55] Laski, pp. 139–40.
[56] Cmd. 6404.
[57] *Crossbow*, Vol. 4, No. 10, pp. 13–14.
[58] Cd. 9230, p. 5.
[59] Muir, p. 113. The author envisaged a 'Supreme Cabinet' of 10, together with a series of 'Sub-Cabinets' for consideration of detailed routine.
[60] Laski, p. 153.
[61] Morrison, p. 56. Stewart in *op. cit.* pp. 45–6 also favours a more restricted Cabinet.
[62] *The Constitutional History of Modern Britain since 1485*, 6th ed., Adam and Charles Black, London 1960, p. 500.
[63] In practice, as is well known, the strong Party organization in Parliament considerably reduces such Ministerial risks.
[64] Cmd. 4060 of 1932.
[65] In Lord Campion and others, p. 233.
[66] D. Foot, H.C. Deb. 295, cs. 693ff.
[67] H. Strauss, H. C. Deb. 330, c. 1264.
[68] Holdsworth: *ibid.*, c. 1279.
[69] Pollard: *How to Reform Parliament*, p. 43.
[70] Carr's statistics. Lord Campion and others, p. 241.
[71] *Contemporary Review*, Vol. CXLIII, February 1933.
[72] *Political Quarterly*, Vol. V, 1934.
[73] Lord Campion and others, p. 251.
[74] *Law and Orders*, 2nd ed., 1956.
[75] *Justice and Administrative Law*, 3rd. ed., 1951.
[76] *The Passing of Parliament*, 2nd ed., 1954.
[77] Lord Campion and others, Chap. XI.
[78] Curtis, p. 108.
[79] H.C. 189 of 1945/6, p. xlv.
[80] *ibid.* p. xli.
[81] See section (*a*), Chapter III.
[82] *Speed up Law Reform*, pp. 24–5.
[83] H.C. 211 of 1956/7.
[84] Cmd. 4060, pp. 67–8.
[85] Lord Campion and others, p. 251.
[86] H.C. 310 of 1952/3, p. xxiv.
[87] *ibid.*, pp. xxiv *passim.*
[88] Lord Campion and others, p. 233.
[89] *ibid.* p. 248.
[90] See Morrison, pp. 248–9.
[91] *ibid.* p. 251.
[92] For an analysis of the various nationalization measures, see Chester, *The Nationalized Industries, A Statutory Analysis*, Allen & Unwin Ltd., 1951.
[93] Morrison, p. 251.
[94] H.C. Deb. 478, cs. 2795–814 (Debate on the Socialized Industries, 25th October 1950).
[95] In Lord Campion and others, p. 266.
[96] H.C. Deb. 451, c. 1635.
[97] H.C. 332 of 1951/2.
[98] *Nationalised Industry I—Accountability to Parliament*, Acton Society Trust, 1950.

[99] H.C. 332 of 1951/2, Q. 458.
[100] Morrison, p. 262.
[101] *ibid.* p. 261.
[102] e.g. Motion, 10th July 1958.
[103] *The Times*, 26th February 1960.
[104] H.C. Deb. 478, c. 2872.
[105] Curtis, p. 123.
[106] H.C. Deb. 478, c. 2806.
[107] H.C. Deb. 478, cs. 2842-3.
[108] H.C. 235 of 1952/3.
[109] H.C. 121 of 1954/5.
[110] H.C. 120 of 1955/6.
[111] H.C. 187 of 1957/8, para. 5.
[112] *The Times*, 13th August 1953.
[113] *Observer*, 16th August 1953.
[114] *Nationalisation in Britain. The End of a Dogma*, Macmillan & Co., Ltd. 1958, Chap. 8.
[115] *The Times*, 30th November 1957.
[116] H.C. Deb. 581, cs. 103-66; 591, cs. 825-946.
[117] H.C. Deb. 617, c. 113.
[118] *Observer*, 16th August 1953.
[119] H.C. 187 of 1957/8 para. 4.
[120] H.C. 276 of 1958/9.
[121] *The Times*, 28th January 1960.
[122] Morrison, pp. 274-5.
[123] In Lord Campion and others, p. 270.
[124] *Reporting to Parliament on the Nationalised Industries*, published by the Royal Institute of Public Administration 1957.
[125] Kelf-Cohen, pp. 161-2.
[126] Morrison, H.C. Deb. 478, c. 2799.
[127] Sir James Bowman, H.C. 304 of 1956/7, p. 128.
[128] In Chapter III, under 'Financial Procedure', section (b).
[129] H.C. 187 of 1957-8, para. 5.
[130] Lord Campion and others, p. 263.
[131] *Parliamentary Affairs*, Vol. XII, pp. 199-208.
[132] *Spectator*, No. 6832, p. 800. There were also articles in the *Observer* of 31st May 1959 and 7th June 1959 on the functions of the Ombudsman.
[133] Up to April 1960 twelve Members had signed the Motion asking for a Select Committee to inquire into the possibility of appointing a 'Parliamentary Commissioner' (Ombudsman).
[134] The Norwegian *Bergens Tidende* of 25th May 1959, announced that the Norwegian Minister of Justice would be bringing in a Bill to establish an Ombudsman in that country, under the heading: 'Safeguards against Bureaucracy'.

VI

Parliament and Public Opinion

(a) PARLIAMENT AND THE PEOPLE

Parliamentary government involves, if not the agreement of the governed, at least their consent; and the preservation of parliamentary institutions rests finally upon the goodwill of the people. As Gilbert Murray once said, if we are to keep the parliamentary system the people must be in a parliamentary frame of mind, must have a respect for Parliament and an interest in public affairs.[1] 'The ultimate sanction of the British Constitution', asserted Carter, 'is found in public opinion.'[2] There is no doubt of the importance of public opinion. It has two aspects: it must not only accept parliamentary institutions if they are to be maintained, it can also exercise direct influence upon the course of Government. This second aspect is of less immediate concern here: it is one of the accepted characteristics and glories of parliamentary government.[3]

It is the first aspect of public opinion—its acceptance of parliamentary forms—which more concerns us here. In this, there is little doubt that the trend of opinion over the last thirty years or so has been one of the happiest features of our public life. It is often a strange experience to read among articles and books on Parliament published in the 1930s. It is typical of the period that Murray should begin the article referred to above by saying that *if* we are to keep our parliamentary institutions certain conditions must be satisfied. The sense that there was a real doubt whether we would, should or could keep our parliamentary institutions runs through many publications of the time. That it should have been so then, and that the situation should have changed since, is understandable. In the 1930s Parliament was seemingly impotent in the face of one overwhelming problem: economic depression,

For Notes and References see pages 159–161

with its harsh consequences in unemployment, poverty, frustration, and waste. At the time it seemed to many that while Hitler, Mussolini and Stalin were showing the way with vigorous economic planning, it was the parliamentary system itself (the 'talking-shop') that hampered similar efforts here. The wane of parliamentary institutions in the Fascist states and, of course, the example of Soviet Russia which had always appealed strongly to people of very left-wing views, together led to insistent questioning of the adequacy of Parliament to cope with modern problems of government. Writing in the *Daily Mail* in April 1935, Winston Churchill said that the preceding decade had been 'disastrous' to parliamentary institutions in almost every part of the world, and he felt obliged to stress that there was no greater guarantee of this country's liberties than the House of Commons. The 'official statement of the proposals of Mosley's New Party' for parliamentary reform which appeared in an article in the *Political Quarterly* in 1931[4] makes strange reading today, as do Stafford Cripps' plan[5] for Government by Order in Council under an enabling Bill. Socialist writers were concerned about the difficult conditions which they would meet if they achieved power, and Cabinet dictatorship—at least for a temporary period—seems to have been widely envisaged as the only way of preventing economic collapse (the fall of the second Labour Government in 1931 was, naturally, always in mind). How different is the situation to-day! It has been said that the basic health of our parliamentary institutions was shown by the fact that they were adequate to the purpose of the Labour Party when it came to power in 1945, with an extremely extensive programme of legislation. No major changes were made or needed to be made.[6] There is no doubt that the experiences of the war[7] and post-war years have completely altered the climate of opinion: the indefinite suspension of parliamentary government is no longer seriously envisaged.

The difference in the attitude of the public towards Parliament in 1945, as compared with what it was in 1931, is summed up in the Third Report of the 1945-6 Select Committee on Procedure. Referring to the work of their predecessors in 1931-2, the Committee reported: 'The atmosphere in which your Committee approach their task is entirely different from that in which the former Committee found themselves. The country was then undergoing a period of severe economic stress . . . and there was a tendency to criticize all the institutions of government, including Parliament itself. . . . Your Committee have been appointed at a time when the country has recently emerged from a war in which parliamentary activity was maintained and contributed in large measure to its successful prosecution. Consequently, there is not at the present time any strong or wide-spread desire for changes in the essential character of the institution. Indeed, the prestige of Parliament has probably never been higher.'[8]

It is difficult for a comparatively young person to speak of public opinion in the 1930s, but it seems that the continued viability of parliamentary institutions was not only in doubt among politicians themselves, writers to *The Times*, and so on, but among many ordinary people as well. Today it is probably true to say that the British Parliament as an institution is generally believed to be well able to discharge its functions. There are few signs of contempt for parliament as a system, or of dissatisfaction with it, however much its particular actions may be criticized. Nor would it be true to say that there is apathy: Parliament is something that is accepted—often accepted, perhaps, with nearly complete ignorance of what it really is or how it works—but accepted along with our systems of coinage and of driving on the left. Support for movements which would involve changing parliamentary government radically—Communism, Fascism—has always been minute.[9]

It is against this reassuring background that the question of possible reforms regarding the relationship between Parliament and the public may be discussed.

(b) PUBLICITY FOR PARLIAMENT

The understanding and informed acceptance of Parliament are aims never finally achieved: for one thing, there is always a new generation. There is no need to rehearse here the achievements of the Hansard Society for Parliamentary Government. But the work of such a body can only reach a comparatively small proportion of the people (though the influence of its publications in universities, schools, W.E.A. classes, etc., may be more extensive). For most people, what they know and understand of Parliament—

and the esteem in which they hold it—depend largely on the organs of mass communication: particularly the radio, television, and the Press.

The effect of radio and television has probably been almost entirely beneficial, so far as spreading a knowledge and understanding of Parliament is concerned. Such popular programmes as 'Any Questions?' in which Members and others discuss informally serious and frivolous topics of the day, generally do an immense amount of good in bringing a fairly wide selection of Members in close contact with millions of people; the same is true of similar television programmes. But there have been problems, some of which remain.

A source of friction in the past in the relation between Parliament and the broadcasting mediums has been the 'Fourteen-Day Rule'. A skeleton account of this affair may be in place here. In 1944, the Governors of the B.B.C. considered the situation which had arisen from a broadcast by the President of the Board of Education on the eve of the Second Reading of the Education Bill in the House of Commons. They resolved that the broadcasting of *ex parte* statements was undesirable at a time when debates on major matters of policy were imminent, and thus brought into play, of their own volition, what came to be known as the Fourteen-Day Rule. After the war, a number of meetings were held in order to re-define the Rule. In the course of these, in 1948, the B.B.C. were prepared to give the assurances:

(i) that they had no intention of becoming an alternative, simultaneous debating forum to Parliament;

(ii) that they would not have discussions on any issues which were to be debated in either House within a fortnight; and

(iii) that while matters were subjects of legislation, M.P.s would not be used in such discussions.

The Rule, however, began to impose some difficulties on the Governors, and the 1949 Broadcasting Committee, reporting in January 1951 (Cmd. 8116), felt that it should be reconsidered. In May 1952, the Government said they would initiate discussions on the point; in March 1953, the B.B.C definitely sought to disengage themselves from the Rule which, they said, imposed great administrative difficulties, and which the public thought absurd. Government and Opposition representatives, on the other hand, attached importance to the Rule being retained; it was desirable to protect M.P.s from undue pressure before a debate from the loud, but single, voice of the B.B.C.

After various exchanges from both sides, the House of Commons debated the issue on 30th November 1955. On a free vote, the House agreed (by 271 votes to 126) to the principle of some limitation, but at the same time set up a Select Committee to see whether any changes were desirable in the way of giving effect to the principle.

The Select Committee reported in May 1956,[10] and their views did not seem wholly compatible with those of the Members who had so clearly endorsed the principle of limitation. The only justification for this limitation, said the Committee, was the necessity of upholding the primacy of Parliament in debating the affairs of the nation: but, with the rapid increase of alternative programmes, even this ground of objection could hardly be regarded as providing anything more than a temporary justification. The Committee recommended that in future the limitation should be, at the most, one of seven days only, and that the ban on discussion of proposed legislation should be altogether removed after a bill had been read the second time.

In December 1956, the Prime Minister was able to announce that the B.B.C. and I.T.A. had agreed that, if the Fourteen-Day Rule was suspended, they would continue to act in a way which would not derogate from the primacy of Parliament as the forum for debating the affairs of the nation.[11] In the light of this, the Fourteen-Day Rule was suspended—at first, for an experimental period, and, later, indefinitely.[12]

There have been, from time to time, several suggestions for the direct broadcasting of Parliament itself. Amery has summarized the aims of one school of thought: 'The real opportunity to my mind of rekindling interest in Parliament . . . is to have Parliament broadcast on a special wavelength throughout the session. . . . I do not believe that this would lead to "talking to the gallery". . . . On the contrary, broadcasting audiences are very critical of anything but sober good sense, and I believe the effect would be definitely to raise the standards of debates and to create an ever-increasing body of parliamentary fans following the proceedings.'[13]

The late Aneurin Bevan advocated broadcasting of the complete proceedings in the House on 30th June 1944. However, the broadcasting of debates was rejected by the Commons on 21st August 1945. A slightly different suggestion—that all proceedings should be recorded—was advanced by King-Hall on 30th June 1944.[14] This also was refused (11th December 1945)—it had been considered 'over and over again' and there was said to be no substantial support for it.[15] Permission to broadcast or record can, of course, come only from the whole House. It is well known that during the war the Prime Minister asked the House to allow his own speeches to be recorded so that they could later be broadcast, thus saving himself precious time and energy. However, he found that the motion to implement the suggestion aroused so much difference of opinion in the House that it was never moved.

The comparatively recent campaign for televising the proceedings of the Commons received support from Bevan at the beginning of the 1959 Parliament. Referring to 'a considerable gulf growing between this House and the nation', and to a general lessening of interest in Parliament, he called for a serious investigation into the technical possibilities of televising parliamentary proceedings. A special channel would be required: viewers should be able to switch over to a debate when they wished to do so.[16] R. A. Butler, replying, confirmed that if this 'revolutionary suggestion' were adopted, then a special channel might well be imperative—since the problem of 'editing' debates would otherwise be bound to arise.[17] The Prime Minister subsequently announced, on 1st March 1960, that from inquiries made by the Government it appeared that the proposal to televise debates did not yet command the support necessary to justify 'so radical a departure from our traditions'.

Television and radio, however, have already been admitted to the Palace of Westminster to cover the State Opening of Parliament, and certain important ceremonies such as the visit of President de Gaulle in the spring of 1960; they are also playing an increasingly prominent part in elections. After the first television by-election,[18] an article by the political correspondent of *The Times* discussed the issues which might arise in the future:[19]

There is little doubt what the television authorities want. They are going to press for the right to treat a General

Election as they treat other first-class news, and to arrange discussion programmes during an election campaign in which the speakers will be something more than the puppets and voices of the Party caucuses. The television authorities, in fact, must be expected to found themselves upon the principle that a General Election cannot be a closed shop for politicians, and that the electorate at large and the commentators have as good a claim to settle what the issues shall be as the politicians. But this large proposition has only to be mentioned to many professional politicians to make them behave like a nervous matron cycling in a high wind, never sure how only two hands may be used to grip the handlebars, hold on to a hat, and keep down a hemline. One calamity or the other is almost certain.

Since this prophecy, the country has experienced a General Election in which coverage by both sound radio and television was very full.

Other suggestions for making Parliament better known to the public have concerned facilities for visitors within the Palace. The Public Gallery in the new House of Commons is considerably larger than that in the old. King-Hall suggested to the Select Committee on House of Commons Rebuilding that one side-gallery should be enclosed in glass and soundproofed.[20] Such a gallery would be particularly useful for organized parties, with an official present to explain proceedings. A further suggestion was that there should be a 'Look-Listen' room accommodating 500 people near the Chamber, where proceedings could be watched on television.

Diana Spearman has pointed to a possible danger in the effect of the use of radio, television, etc., in politics.[21] She says that 'the back-bencher remains a back-bencher even in his own constituency' —the Press, radio and television enable the Party leaders to address the public over the heads of local Members. At the moment, the complaint can to some extent be borne out by the fact that we have, in this country, no network of local radio stations as there is in America. But a network of local television stations is being developed and these may well go some way towards restoring a fairer balance. The local candidates, and not the Party leaders, had the limelight at the first televised by-election in Rochdale, and Granada TV's 'Election Marathon' of 1959 was an experiment in *constituency* television: 229 candidates contesting 100 northern constituencies appeared. Ed Murrow said of this 'operation' that it had the laudable aim of *not* concentrating too much on the national political figures. We may one day reach a situation similar to that in America, where local political issues and personalities are reported at length by the different local stations, with occasional 'national' programmes by the Party leaders relayed by every station.

The Select Committee on Broadcasting in 1956 brought to light another aspect of the relationship between Parliament and the public. Sir Robert (now Lord) Boothby averred that the Party machines interfered with the ordinary programmes of the B.B.C. and I.T.V., and that this was undesirable.[22] He quoted a statement in a book by a former Chairman of the B.B.C., in which it is said that the leaders of the political Parties objected to the employment in B.B.C. programmes of Members who were not 'reliable' Party men;[23] the B.B.C.'s dilemma came from the fact that many of the 'extreme' politicians made the best broadcasters. It was also claimed that a particular M.P. was debarred from appearing in a sports broadcast because, in any radio programme, each M.P. had to be balanced by a member of the other main party.[24] The spokesmen for the political parties and the B.B.C. denied that there had been any improper dealings on the subject. The Director-General of the B.B.C. explained that it was not in any way their policy to build up political personalities and give them a spurious standing.[25] The party spokesman said that the pressure they exerted was solely designed towards ensuring a reasonable balance of political views.[26] The Committee were satisfied that the charges were unfounded, and that the B.B.C. was quite able to defend itself from political interference.[27]

The extent to which M.P.s have been able to stamp an image on the public consciousness by means of broadcasting and television, over a given period, was shown in a Written Answer to a Parliamentary Question in 1956.[28] This gave the table on page 151.

The Press is still a vitally important medium for the dissemination of information and comment about Parliament, despite the

Year	Total number of broadcasts featuring M.P.s	Total number of M.P.s concerned	Number of M.P.s who have broadcast 6 or more times
1948	235	124	5
1949	210	114	5
1950	226	100	8
1951	376	123	20
1952	396	150	17
1953	359	132	15
1954	366	147	16
1955 to 31st October	330	135	14

I.T.A.: APPEARANCES OF MEMBERS OF PARLIAMENT — JANUARY TO SEPTEMBER, 1957 (INCLUSIVE), (EXCLUDING NEWS PROGRAMMES AND PARTY POLITICAL BROADCASTS)

Month	Conservative	Labour	Liberal
January	11	8	–
February	15	12	–
March	13	10	–
April	14	7	–
May	14	8	1
June	2	6	–
July	3	10	–
August	3	6	–
September	3	8	2
TOTAL ..	78	75	3

The number of M.P.s, as distinct from appearances, is not available.

growing significance of television, and even allowing for the fact that popular newspapers can normally afford but a modest space for parliamentary and political matters. Grimond has distinguished three essential roles played by the Press in relation to Parliament:

Subsequently, the following information—for television only—was given to the House of Commons by the Postmaster-General:[29]

NUMBER OF M.P.S AND APPEARANCES ON B.B.C. TELEVISION FROM 1st APRIL, 1956—31st MARCH, 1958

(excluding news programmes and party political broadcasts)

Date	Conservative	Number of broadcasts	Labour	Number of broadcasts	Liberal	Number of broadcasts	Independent	Number of broadcasts
1 April–30 June 1956	6	6	7	13	–	–	–	–
1 July–30 Sept. 1956	6	6	4	4	1	1	–	–
1 Oct.–31 Dec. 1956	15	17	8	9	2	2	–	–
1 Jan.–31 March 1957	10	13	13	15	–	–	1	1
TOTAL	32*	42	25*	41	2*	3	1	1
1 April–30 June 1957	8	9	10	12	–	–	–	–
1 July–30 Sept. 1957	9	9	9	11	1	2	1	1
1 Oct.–31 Dec. 1957	12	13	9	13	1	1	–	–
1 Jan.–31 March 1958	14	17	11	11	1	1	–	–
TOTAL	35*	48	28*	47	2*	4	1	1

*These figures represent the total number of M.P.s who have appeared in the year. Several Members have appeared in more than one quarter; hence, the 'totals' do not necessarily correspond with the figures in the columns above.

it interprets the country to Parliament: it interprets Parliament to the country; and it is itself a 'third Chamber' by virtue of its own discussions. Grimond points to the value of the independent, reasoned reports and articles in *The Times*, the *Guardian* and certain other newspapers which tend to treat problems from a national point of view; at the same time, he deplores our present dearth of political commentators of high standing.[30] More recently Bevan castigated much newspaper reporting as 'sheer travesty'; but this seems to be an extreme view.[31]

Relations between Parliament and the Press are not always happy, as the last remark shows. There is a long, well known history of jealousy between these two institutions, both competing for the claim to be the decisive *vox populi*. Even to-day, the reporting of Parliament is technically a breach of privilege. A particular cause of friction recently has been the reporting of 'secret' Party meetings. The subject was gone into at length by the Committee of Privileges with reference to the Garry Allighan Case.[32] In an article, 'Parliament and Press', H. G. Nicholas pointed out the 'impossibility' of the situation:[33] journalists can only print news of such Party meetings when what is supposed to be secret information is divulged to them. Nicholas proposed, as a remedy, that Party meetings should no longer be secret—at least not all of them.[34] An instance of similar friction occurred in March 1958. Arthur Lewis then raised the question of a report in certain newspapers, which claimed that two rooms in the Palace where Party meetings were held had been searched for hidden microphones—as part of an intensive effort to solve the mystery of how 'accurate verbatim accounts' of 'secret' meetings had reached the Press.[35] The whole question of such 'secret' meetings cannot be said to have been happily solved to date.

(c) THE MEMBER AND HIS CONSTITUENTS

The relationship between an M.P. and his constituents has already been partly considered in Chapters I and IV. Nigel Nicolson has pointed out how contradictory are the demands made on M.P.s by their constituents.[36] The Member is constantly being pressed to voice the views or needs of special interests, and these may easily be in conflict with his own conception of the national interest and of his duties as someone who is more than the 'delegate' of his constituents.

It is occasionally argued that one reason why, if practicable, the Commons should sit for a lesser part of the year is that Members would then have improved opportunities to develop their contacts with the people—above all, of course, with their constituents. The extent to which an M.P. should devote himself to 'constituency interests' has attracted much attention of late. The term does not apply so much to the major, collective problems of any given area—a Member must (and invariably does) devote his time selflessly to such things as growing local unemployment, general lack of housing, flood disasters, etc.—as to the countless *individual* worries of the constituents. In other words, how far should the Member regard himself as a welfare officer? Should he spend much time investigating whether Mrs. X's son was dismissed from his job without proper notice, or whether Mr. Y's daughter's adverse school report was fair comment on the latter's abilities? A distinguished opponent of excessive 'surgery' work is Lord Attlee, who contends that in these days of legal aid, Citizens' Advice Bureaux and similar institutions, a Member should not be bothered with such a mass of detailed work—to the detriment of his duties in Parliament.[37] Lord Winterton has voiced similar comments.[38] The idea that M.P.s should be paid 'a whacking salary and then become full-time constituency welfare officers' does not appeal to Philip Goodhart.[39] Yet there is a strong current of informed opinion that it would be undesirable for a Member to cut himself off from this work—however weary, stale and unprofitable it may sometimes be.[40] To whom is the constituent with a genuine personal grievance to turn, if not to his Member? Moreover, the latter can, should and does refer many of such inquiries and complaints to the 'appropriate authorities'. There is no doubt that an M.P.'s 'welfare' services are sometimes abused, and precious time wasted in consequence; yet to many the alternative seems even less acceptable, and would scarely improve relations between Parliament and the public.

This responsibility to his constituents adds heavily to an already busy man's work, and it is small wonder that there is to-day substantial agreement that at the very least 250 full-time Members are now required in the House.[41] For, apart from constituency responsibilities, the duties of Members at Westminster *outside* the actual Chamber have multiplied with the increase in Committee work (and in other work besides)—to an extent which only the Members concerned are in a position to assess accurately. At the same time, it must be conceded that critics of 'too many professional politicians' have not been slow to speak up. In some quarters there undoubtedly exists an apparently innate preference for the man who combines his duties at Westminster with an outside profession. There are, of course, certain serious motives for this preference. It is felt that the Member entirely dependent on his parliamentary salary may feel disinclined to speak against his Party's policy, since expulsion from the Party could easily entail the loss of his seat. The other reason is the desirability of keeping Parliament in close touch with the country as a whole; it is argued, very plausibly, that to achieve this contact at least a proportion of Members must not be full-time politicians. Otherwise, asked *The Times*, how can the House of Commons remain the microcosm of the nation?[42] The ideal, widely accepted solution, of course, is that the composition of the House should strike a happy balance between full-time Members and those who are able to combine their parliamentary duties with an outside profession. Both forms of service are essential to the modern parliamentary machine; and public opinion, generally speaking, accepts the fact.[43]

The major contentious issue of recent times, in this particular context, has been the extent to which a Member is bound to follow the known wishes of his constituents and, in particular, of his local association. The reader is referred to Chapter IV for consideration of this question.

(d) PARLIAMENTARY PRIVILEGE

The assertion of parliamentary privilege seems to run increases in Members' pay a close second in its ability to render public opinion towards Parliament hostile. A note on the subject is therefore in place here.

The notion that parliamentary privilege works for the benefit of the common people is perhaps rather too difficult for many people to grasp.[44] There have also been some cases in recent years in which the claims of Members for protection have appeared, to many, to border on the absurd; these claims may have caught the public attention, while the contemptuous rejection of them by the House may have gone unnoticed. The sensible position on this matter has been stated by the Committee of Privileges itself:[45]

> Your Committee are of the opinion that it is not consistent with the dignity of the House that penal proceedings for breach of privilege should be taken in the case of every defamatory statement which, strictly, may constitute a contempt of Parliament. Whilst recognizing that it is the duty of Parliament to intervene in the case of attacks which may tend to undermine public confidence in and support of the institution of Parliament itself, your Committee think it important that, on the one hand, the law of Parliamentary Privilege should not be administered in a way which would fetter or discourage the free expression of opinion or criticisms, however prejudiced or exaggerated such opinions or criticisms may be; and that, on the other hand, the process of Parliamentary investigation should not be used in a way which would give importance to impossible statements.[46]

The question of whether the Committee of Privileges has been right or wrong in its assessment of particular cases is not relevant here. There have been, however, some suggestions recently for reform of the way in which alleged breaches of privileges are dealt with. An unsigned article appearing in *The Times* of 27th March 1957 stated an opinion which has since received a good deal of support. The writer pointed out that the House of Commons is not, in law, a court, and is not, in practice, adapted to the exercise of functions of a judicial nature. A recognition of this fact led in 1868 to the transfer from the House to the courts of jurisdiction over disputed elections. The writer goes on to suggest that this course could be followed in matters of privilege also. The basis of the rules which relate to breach of privilege is clear enough— whether an alleged breach tends to obstruct the functioning of the House. This is a question with which the courts could well cope. The writer suggested that it would be better for the dignity of Parliament if affronts to its authority were either clearly seen to be assessed in accordance with judicial standards, or else ignored as unworthy of notice.

In the ensuing correspondence, O. Hood Phillips suggested a distinction between cases of privilege, with which the House is necessarily concerned, which are recognized by the courts, and which may not be extended, and cases of contempt which are incapable of enumeration, and which might well be triable only in the courts.[47] B. E. H. Amps pointed out that those investigated by the Committee of Privileges had no right to defend themselves, or to be heard, or to make public their defence.[48] He suggested that procedure could be devised similar to that of courts by which the accused had the right of hearing by the Committee, and by which the House and the public should hear both sides of the case. Clearly, public interest had been aroused. On 10th April 1957, six Conservative Members tabled a motion which read: 'That it be an instruction to the Committee of Privileges, *in view of the prevailing public uncertainty and anxiety on the matter*, to prepare and submit to the House a report which shall define the nature and clarify the purpose of parliamentary privilege; and recommend a procedure designed to secure its equitable protection.'

The later stages of the 'Strauss' case have led to several repetitions of the suggestion that jurisdiction in matters of privilege should be transferred to the courts.[49] The outcome of the question of privilege raised by G. R. Strauss, M.P. for Vauxhall, caused some anxiety to a number of Members. If the 'Strauss'[50] letter was *not* covered by privilege (as the House decided by a small majority), were Members likely to be involved in libel actions if they followed up constituency grievances? A group of Labour Members subsequently asked for an extension of Question Time, to accommodate business that was conducted formerly by correspondence. It has been suggested that the proper means of dealing with grievances which might involve libel action is for the Member to forward them to the Minister with the simple addition of a 'compliments' slip. The matter was raised on 16th March 1954, when Winston Churchill added that the M.P. might be well advised to ask his correspondent whether he would be willing for the letter to be disclosed to a wider circle.[51] Sir H. Lucas-Tooth has proposed that the Member should ask the complainant whether he would object to his letter being forwarded to the person against whom the charge is made.[52] All this takes us some way from the specific question of privilege, as it affects Parliament's relations with the public, but it serves to show the importance and the complexity of the issues raised by the 'Strauss' case. As had been pointed out, the threat of the London Electricity Board to proceed against Mr. Strauss came as a shock to a wide body of parliamentary opinion.[53]

There, for the moment, the matter rests. Many of those who have recently argued that procedure in dealing with alleged breaches of privilege should be amended, have explicitly advanced the point that the present system—in which the House is at once (so it is said) prosecutor, judge and jury—has lowered the esteem in which Parliament is held. Certainly, however, the principle of privilege in itself has not been attacked by those informed observers (few though they may be) who grasp its true significance and function.

Conclusions

In the recent debate on the matter of privilege which he had raised, Strauss said:[54] 'While there is a deep respect in this country for Parliament as an institution there is, unfortunately, not the same respect for the Members who compose it.' The 'unfortunately' is rather gratuitous. It is true that public opinion does not accord automatically an exaggerated degree of respect to Members. This is, perhaps, not a matter for regret, and those who argue that things were different in earlier days produce little evidence to support their case. The idea that harsh, often unfair criticisms were *not* levelled at Members in 'the good old days' is in fact completely erroneous.[55] 'As the franchise became more democratic', observed Winston Churchill in the Commons on 27th February 1941, 'it grew to be the fashion in certain social circles to speak with contempt about Members as a class and as a type. They were represented as mere spouters and chatterboxes, the putters of awkward questions and the raisers of small points of procedure.' Members can at best expect to win the general public's respect according to their abilities and merits, and cannot count on receiving respect merely, as it were, *ex officio*. There is a genuine distinction, however, between Parliament, and the Members who at any one time compose it; and Strauss is surely right in saying that there is in this country today a deep respect for Parliament itself. The continuance of this respect, a pre-

158

requisite of parliamentary government, is not an end and aim that can be pursued by itself. It is a by-product: something that must depend on the ability of Parliament to discharge its traditional functions in continually changing circumstances. The problems raised by these changes have been discussed in the present and preceding chapters; the attitude of public opinion towards Parliament may well depend upon the efficacy of the solutions adopted.

The chances are, however, that Parliament will long remain the people's hope. Professor André Mathiot has written an interesting, sympathetic account of *The British Political System*.[56] In it, he deals with the various aspects of our Constitution. His conclusion reveals how he, a foreigner, appreciates the vital, intimate inter-relation between that Constitution and the British people at large: describing the system as 'an enviable model of democratic government', he adds that 'one can only regret that it could not possibly be transplanted to any other country'.[57] Could it be that Winston Churchill summed up the whole situation in 1908 when he described the British Constitution (of which Parliament is the centre-point) as 'mainly British common sense'?[58]

NOTES AND REFERENCES

[1] *Contemporary Review*, Vol. CXLI, 1932, pp. 296–308.

[2] Carter, p. 198.

[3] Of course, the exercise of public opinion is no simple matter in a highly organized country of 50 million people with centralized organs of mass communication such as the Press, radio, television, political parties, trades unions, and so on. Everything from a letter to *The Guardian* signed by, say, 200 members of the academic staff of London University, to a report of a resolution by a local branch of the T. and G.W.U., plays its part in the whole complicated story. The organs of communication play a double part in both expressing, and helping to form, opinion.

[4] Vol. II, pp. 319–36.

[5] *Political Quarterly*, Vol. IV, 1933, pp. 467–81.

[6] R. Bassett, 'British Parliamentary Government today', in *Political Quarterly*, Vol. XXIII, 1952, pp. 380–89; cf. also Crick, p. 1.

[7] It is true that Governments had exceptional powers in these years—but these powers were granted by Parliament, were subject to parliamentary scrutiny and questioning, and were gradually diminished. The extent of these powers was a legitimate subject for Party differences, but it was seldom suggested that they were necessarily inimical to the parliamentary system. Ed Murrow, in a famous broadcast, said: 'Do you remember that while London was being bombed in daylight, the House devoted two days to discussing conditions under which enemy aliens were detained on the Isle of Man?'

(Quoted by K. R. Mackenzie in *The English Parliament*, revised and reprinted, Penguin Books, 1959).

[8] H.C. 189–I of 1945/6, p.v.

[9] A subject that is raised from time to time is how much better things would be if we could have a government of wise men, instead of the parliamentary battle. Sir Hartley (now Lord) Shawcross gave the subject an airing when he said that a committee of ten sensible men of goodwill could accomplish in a couple of hours what may occupy the time of Parliament for a couple of days. (*The Times*, 23rd December 1957, p. 4.) He might have said 'a couple of years' and the remark could still have been perfectly true. Remarks such as these, which when considered are seen to strike at the roots of the parliamentary system, seldom receive wide support. And, after all, the parliamentary system already contains within it a committee of ten (or twenty) sensible men of goodwill—the Cabinet. The men of goodwill envisaged by Shawcross could only achieve more than the Cabinet if they were unfettered by parliamentary control—if they had, in fact, dictatorial and not parliamentary power.

[10] H.C. 288 of 1955/6: Broadcasting (Anticipation of Debates) Select Committee Report.

[11] H.C. Deb. 562, cs. 1095–7.

[12] H.C. Deb. 574, cs. 91–2W. (25th July 1957).

[13] Amery, p. 56.

[14] H.C. Deb. 401, c. 976.

[15] H.C. Deb. 417, cs. 213–4.

[16] H.C. Deb. 612, cs. 865–67.

[17] H.C. Deb. 612, c. 972.

[18] Ably documented in the pamphlet *Granada goes to Rochdale* published by Granada Television, 1958.

[19] 23rd June 1958, p. 6.

[20] H.C. 109–I of 1943/4, p. 139.

[21] Spearman, p. 167.

[22] H.C. 288 of 1955/6.

[23] The late Lord Simon of Wythenshawe: *The B.B.C. from Within*, Gollancz, Ltd., 1956, p. 133.

[24] H.C. 288 of 1955/6, p. 165.

[25] *ibid*. Q. 184.

[26] *ibid*. p. iv.

[27] *ibid*.

[28] H.C. Deb. 546, c. 174. W.

[29] H.C. Deb. 588, cs. 394–6.

[30] In Watson, pp. 47–8.

[31] H.C. Deb. 612, c. 865.

[32] H.C. 138 of 1946/7. Allighan's 'contempt' was based on an article in which he said that some M.P.s disclosed confidential information to newspapers in return for financial reward or personal publicity.

[33] *Nineteenth Century and After*, Vol. CXLIII, pp. 249–55.

[34] The case against the secrecy of Party meetings is also argued on other grounds: see Chapter IV, section (*b*).

[35] H.C. Deb. 584, cs. 924–6.

[36] *People and Parliament*, Chap. I.

[37] *Fabian Journal*, November 1958, p. 6.

[38] In a letter to *The Times*, 15th April 1957, p. 11.

[39] *Crossbow*, Vol. III, No. 10, pp. 10–11.

[40] e.g. Crick, pp. 9–11 ('The Constituency Case'); and Donnelly, *The Times*, 17th April 1957, p. 11.

[41] From 250 to 300, according to Lord Attlee: *The Times*, 11th April 1957, p. 11. The Select Committee on Procedure (H.C. 92 of 1958/9: Proceedings, p. lii) recognized the growing tendency in recent years 'to divide Members into what are called "whole-time parliamentarians" and those "with outside interests".'

[42] 17th January 1958, p. 11.

[43] The distinction between these two 'forms' of Membership, as has been rightly emphasized, is artificial, and is made in the present context purely for convenience of discussion. For a categorical rejection of this distinction, see the (narrowly defeated) paragraph brought up and read before the 1958/9 Procedure Committee: H.C. 92 of 1958/9, pp. lii–liii.

[44] 'In its famous protestation . . . in 1621, the Commons declared the Privileges of Parliament to be the birthright and inheritance of the subject. In principle, the Privilege of Parliament is designed to protect a Member's constituents, since without Privilege grievances would be harder to remedy and abuses less likely to be uncovered.' R. A. Butler, H.C. Deb. 591, c. 217.

[45] A statement that compares very favourably with the comments of *The Times* (leader of 23rd December 1957): 'Members' fussiness about their privilege may well be a reflex action. They know that the standing of Parliament in the nation is not what it ought to be and they seek to enforce respect for it. A different mental deportment . . . would be far more effective.'

[46] H.C. 112 of 1947/8, p. iv.

[47] *The Times*, 1st April 1957.

[48] *ibid.* 16th April 1957.

[49] For example, the *Spectator*, 16th May 1958, pp. 611–12. There was a considerable correspondence in *The Times* in July 1958 arising from the debate on the Strauss case.

[50] Richards has summarized the main issues involved in *op. cit.* pp. 262–7. The House debated the matter on 8th July 1958. (H.C. Deb. 591, cs. 208–346.)

[51] H.C. Deb. 525, cs. 210–11.

[52] In a letter to *The Times*, 10th July 1958.

[53] Richards, p. 267.

[54] H.C. Deb. 591, c. 246.

[55] Mr. T. C. Pannell has brought out this point on a number of occasions; e.g. his letter to *The Times*, 3rd January 1958.

[56] Translated by Jennifer S. Hines, Hogarth Press, 1958.

[57] *ibid.*, p. 335.

[58] At the Kinnaird Hall, Dundee, 14th May 1908; cf. G. M. Trevelyan, quoted by Lord Elton (Ramsay Muir Memorial Lecture, 1959): 'The English Parliament . . . was the natural outcome, through long centuries, of the commonsense and the good nature of the English people. . . .'

VII

Parliamentary Life

INTRODUCTION

Criticism of the amenities offered by the Palace of Westminster, and of the way such amenities are controlled, has increased very considerably since the war; and this despite the fact that opportunity was taken, at the time of the re-building of the House of Commons, to provide more accommodation than the pre-war House had allowed.[1] It is now sometimes said that the poor accommodation detracts from the efficiency of Parliament's work; there is also the wider implication that able people are deterred from seeking a career in Parliament because the conditions of life there are so unattractive.

The chief criticisms made are of the lack of accommodation, and the method in which the rooms are allocated for use; the way officers and officials are chosen and controlled; the lack of those amenities which would make life more tolerable and Members' labours more productive; the unavoidable expenses of being a Member, and the insufficient salary.

The remedy proposed by Maxton—that Parliament should move to Hampstead—does not seem to have been weightily considered.

(a) ACCOMMODATION

Mrs. Barbara Castle has called the Palace of Westminster a 'neo-Gothic monstrosity',[2] and it is incontestable that the inadequate nature of the accommodation provided for individual Members within its walls has been constantly adverted to in the post-war years.[3] At first, Government spokesmen countered these complaints

For Notes and References see pages 172–173

by referring to the increased space that would be available when the new Chamber of the House of Commons was built.[4] A Joint Committee, sitting in 1945, had recommended that Sir Charles Barry's original proposal for buildings around New Palace Yard should be reconsidered as a long-term project.[5] A Ministry of Works spokesman, discussing this in 1951, listed the scheme's drawbacks, and preferred to look forward to a new building which was to be erected in Abingdon Street.[6] The attractions and advantages of realizing the 'great and grandiose' Barry scheme, together with a claim that the names of at least one hundred M.P.s in support of such a plan could soon be collected, were again voiced in the Accommodation debate of 31st March 1960.

A Select Committee in the Commons, set up to meet the continuing criticisms of lack of space, recommended that a long waiting-room should be built over the arcade on the east side of New Palace Yard.[7] Desks should be provided for a limited number of Members. The Speaker's Library (one large room) should be made available to Members, thus reducing over-crowding in the Commons Library itself. It was clear to the Committee, however, that whilst minor improvements could be carried out at once, no substantial progress could be made except by large building operations.

These two Reports, and the extensive evidence given by witnesses before the Committee, present a fascinating picture of the inconvenience of life in the Palace of Westminster in the 1950s. (This was perhaps the only Select Committee that has ever discussed, *inter alia*, the shortcomings of the accommodation provided by the House of Commons' mortuary.)[8] The picture afforded by the above Reports (the Committee is most often called the 'Stokes' Committee after its late Chairman) has since been very fully supplemented by the full-dress debate on House of Commons Accommodation held on 31st March 1960.[9] Opinions voiced in that debate included expressions of satisfaction with the House's present facilities, but emphasis was undoubtedly laid by the majority of speakers on the need for vastly improved accommodation. Subsequently, the Minister of Works has made available to Members a scale-model of his proposed alterations and improvements to the Palace of Westminster.

(b) THE CONTROL OF ACCOMMODATION

The Palace of Westminster is in the charge of a Court official, the Lord Great Chamberlain, and he allocates the accommodation in it by warrant to the different users, who make their own detailed distributions. For the House of Lords, this is done by the Lord Great Chamberlain through the Yeoman Usher of the Black Rod. For the Commons it is done on behalf of the Speaker (a) by the Ministry of Works in respect of Ministers' Rooms, and (b) by the Serjeant at Arms in respect of other rooms.

The 1945 Joint Committee rejected the suggestion that this system should be drastically altered;[10] but over a hundred members subsequently supported a motion that the Lord Great Chamberlain's powers should be transferred to a Joint Committee of both Houses;[11] whilst the Commons Select Committee in 1953 expressed the belief that the existing system tended to frustrate or delay desirable changes.[12] As a first step, the Stokes Committee supported the suggestion made by the Joint Committee eight years before, that a sessional 'House' Committee should be appointed to advise the Speaker on the allocation of the rooms at his disposal.[13] The House of Lords already had such a Committee, and it was thought that the two Committees could sit together when it was necessary to discuss matters of mutual concern. It was desirable, the Committee believed, that a unified control of the whole Palace could be exercised. An amendment, repeating this point, to the draft Report of the Select Committee on Procedure in 1958/9, was narrowly defeated.[14] The subject was yet again discussed in the Accommodation debate of 31st March 1960. On that occasion Barbara Castle, speaking from the Opposition front bench, begged to move that 'this House . . . believes that the time has come to implement the proposal of the Select Committee on House of Commons Accommodation, 1953–4, for the establishment of a unified control of the Palace of Westminster under this House; and is, therefore, of the opinion that a House of Commons Commission should be appointed forthwith with the powers and duties proposed in the Select Committee Report, including the consideration of the machinery required to establish such unified control'. Pannell has gone further; he has questioned the whole right of a Court official to operate at Westminster at all, and has drawn attention to the inefficiency which has sprung from 'the amiable fiction that the workshop at Westminster is a royal palace'.[15]

(c) OFFICERS AND OFFICIALS OF THE HOUSE OF COMMONS

The fear that some appointments to the staff of the House might have been made on grounds other than those of merit was considerably dispelled by the Select Committee on House of Commons Accommodation, reporting in 1954.[16] The Committee, however, recommended that the powers at present exercised by the Commissioners for regulating the offices of the House of Commons— a statutory body, consisting largely of Ministers—should be exercised in future by a body of Members. (This suggestion has had the recent support of, amongst others, Barbara Castle.)[17] The 1954 Committee recommended also that a certain over-staffing of the Clerk's department was desirable, in order to deal adequately with peak requirements.

A number of suggestions have been made from time to time that Committees of the House should have their own research staffs, or specialized assistance of some kind. The House has been slow, however, to act in this matter. For a study of the possibilities open, the reader should consult the Special Report from the Select Committee on Nationalized Industries (Reports and Accounts) in 1959.[18]

(d) THE LIBRARY OF THE HOUSE OF COMMONS

An account of the history of the House of Commons Library, which dates from 1818, appeared in the second Report of the Select Committee on House of Commons Accommodation &c.[19] Like most most parliamentary libraries, its duties are keyed to the complicated, changing needs of the legislature it exists to serve, and as individual Members themselves vary in the type and scope of services they expect, unanimity on this last point would be hard to arrive at.

Since the Reports of the Select Committee on the Library in 1945/6, considerable changes in organization and staffing have taken place.[20] A large number of indexes and similar aids enable quick reference to be made to the various sources of information required by Members. The main card catalogues have been over-hauled. There is an International Affairs Desk, an improved Reference Room service, and, in general, better sources of documentation. There is also a small Research Department which undertakes, within its limits, general and statistical work for Members. The senior Library staff is at present (June 1961) composed of ten graduate Library Clerks, in addition to the Librarian.

The debate of 31st March 1960 on House of Commons Accommodation contained a number of references to the Library. Undoubtedly, the main improvements proposed on that occasion in the latter's services to Members concerned a possible extension of its research services. Barbara Castle, emphasizing that the present-day House of Commons was a very important 'workshop',[21] suggested that it was time for 'a quite different approach' to the kind of research and briefing facilities which the modern Member should have: 'Are we not setting our sights too low?'[22]

This point was elaborated by several subsequent speakers in the debate of 31st March 1960, in different directions. The most ambitious scheme was that an enlarged research staff should be able to check and, if necessary, challenge on behalf of the House facts and figures put out by the Government.[23] Such an expansion would bring the Library's services closely into line with those afforded to the United States Congress by the Washington Legislative Reference Service, and opposition to this considerable development was expressed by several speakers in the debate on the grounds of constitutional differences between this country and the United States. There were, however, a number of other pleas for at least some extension in the amount and type of research facilities available to Members—R. A. Butler, winding up on behalf of the Government, undertook to 'attempt to improve the situation' to the best of his ability.[24]

Prior to the 1960 debate on Accommodation, as is well known, a number of outside writers had urged that the House of Commons Library should extend its services to Members—particularly in the matter of its research facilities. But this whole question is at present unsettled, and its solution uncertain. One has to take into account the vastly differing demands and interests of individual

M.P.s. Thus, whilst a strong body of opinion regards opposition to 'bigger research staffs' as similar to opposition to 'motherhood or virtue',[25] voices are still raised either in praise of the present Library services to Members, or else in condemnation of any extension of those services on the grounds of expense and/or constitutional propriety (cf., e.g., the Estimates Committee's Report on the Library: H.C. 168 of 1960/1).

(e) AMENITIES

(i) *Secretaries*. The provision of free secretarial assistance to Members of Parliament has been often suggested. Acland[26] and Pollard[27] both supported the idea during the war. It was considered by the Select Committee on Members' Expenses,[28] who, however, preferred to recommend that there should be a straight increase in salary, rather than an allowance, disguised or open, to cover secretarial assistance; *The Times* criticized this decision in an article head-lined 'A Bad Business'.[29] More recently, the provision of free secretarial facilities has been adverted to by Crick[30] and Nicolson.[31] Barbara Castle has asked that a central remote-control dictation system should be provided for Members; Members would record letters over the telephone, and secretaries would subsequently type them at their convenience. This would afford 'a continuous flow of efficient office output for very little expense'.[32]

(ii) *Post Office Charges*. A suggestion that Members should be allowed to frank their letters (in view of the increasing interest taken by citizens in the work of Parliament, and hence of Members' considerably augmented correspondence), was turned down in 1936.[33] But the proposal has been repeated since on various occasions—for example, to a Select Committee in 1954.[34] Wedgwood Benn has pointed out that Members cannot even communicate freely with each other.[35]

The above Committee of 1954 also heard a suggestion that Members should be allowed to make free trunk-calls to their constituencies.

(iii) *Other Suggested Amenities*. Amongst other suggestions of detail made to the Select Committee on Members' Expenses (too

numerous to consider here at length) were the provision of free
stationery, of living accommodation for Members at a reasonable
cost, and of a limited number of free travel-vouchers for a
Member's wife. An information service, for the speedy answering
of smaller technical problems put by constituents to Members,
has also been suggested;[36] Leslie Hale thought that a teleprinter
service direct to the various Departments might contribute to
that end.[37] Barbara Castle, amongst others, has said that each
Member ought to have his own telephone on his own desk.[38]

(iv) *A Committee on Amenities*. To control these amenities, and
to keep a constant eye open for their improvement, the suggestion
that there should be a Commons 'House' Committee has been
made, and noted above. The House of Lords already has such a
body, and a Joint Committee in 1945 recommended that the
Commons, could, with profit, create one.[39] This suggestion was
later repeated by individual Members[40] and then, in 1953, by the
Select Committee on House of Commons Accommodation.[41]

It might be that the Select Committee on Accommodation which
was set up in 1955, was designed to meet these demands. In that
case, its poor attendances and early demise seem to indicate that
Members, as a whole, were not totally confident that it could do
a useful job of work. Charles Pannell has since said that the
Committee had found its terms of reference and its powers far
too narrow.[42] The latest development along these lines is the
setting up, by Mr. Speaker, of an *ad hoc* Committee of Members
with the following terms of reference:

> To consider the proposals to improve the accommodation
> for Members in the House of Commons set forth in the Min-
> ister of Works' statement (*Hansard*, 31st March 1960, col.
> 1522) and, in particular, the proposal to convert the roof
> space over the Committee Rooms into office accommodation,
> and to make recommendations.[43]

(*f*) MEMBERS' PAY, ETC.

Members' pay[44] is not a subject about which much objective
thinking takes place; it periodically lurches into the public's
attention, but only when Members themselves have been forced

to raise the matter (as a result, generally, of some privation in their midst). Hence, few long-term proposals are made on the subject; and argument, both inside and outside the House, is generally confined to the circumstances of a particular time, and the merits of a particular proposed increase. The situation is complicated by the fact that the issue has to be decided, publicly, by Members themselves; the decisions are taken subject to personal pressures and inhibitions: it could be that an impartial assessor would reach a different conclusion.

This question also raises the much wider issue—discussed in Chapter IV—of how far the House should be composed of 'professional' politicians, and how far of Members pursuing another (outside) profession. Suggestions that whole-time Members should receive higher pay than the others, or that a fee should be paid to Members attending Committees of the House, have been heard.[45] Goodhart has said specifically that chairmen of committees ought to be paid at least £500 a year over and above their parliamentary salaries.[46]

One point of general principle which the House has had to decide has been whether it would be better to have a certain fixed salary, or to have a lower salary with an expense allowance claimable in addition. Here the House decided, as the Select Committee had done previously,[47] that a flat salary was better.[48] In this respect, they ran counter to the views of several writers to *The Times*, who felt it would be more equitable if their legislators received a small fixed sum, above which they would have to argue with the Inland Revenue in order to establish whether their expenses had been wholly and necessarily incurred in their parliamentary duties.[49] *The Times* itself said, in a leader,[50] that an allowance for secretarial help and postage, on top of a small fixed salary, was the better arrangement; Crick agrees that the first thing to be done is to separate the question of salary from that of expenses.[51] But, as stated above, the Committee preferred to recommend a flat, inclusive salary, and the House has since endorsed this principle.

It is often suggested that an increase in salary should be paid to Members only when they can establish that they are in need of it;[52] but the employment of a means test of this kind has never seemed as popular inside the House as outside it. Other ideas voiced have proposed that parliamentary salaries should be fixed by referendum,[53] and that Members should not be allowed any increase in salary until they had presented themselves to the electorate for re-election.[54]

Argument is often caused by the reasons which Members of Parliament advance to justify a particular salary increase. In 1954, the rise in the cost of living was said to require reflection in Members' salaries; but *The Times* objected to this. If the increased cost of living was to be the precedent for raising salaries, it was said, 'the gulf between "we" and "they", which is one of the constant dangers of democracy, will grow'.[55]

Perhaps the simplest and most discreet method of adjusting Members' salaries, as and when necessary, was advocated in a letter to *The Times* by W. Pickles.[56] He stressed the virtues of the French system, which he believed should be mirrored here, under which Members would be tied to the salary level of a particular category of Civil Servants. In this country the Whitley Council would decide when a change in Members' salary was needed; changes would take place without fuss or publicity, though the facts would be ascertainable by the public.

Another type of financial proposal should be mentioned. Acland suggested that a Member's salary should continue for life;[57] Ross, that an unseated Member should be compensated by payment for a period of up to three years.[58] The Select Committee on Members' Expenses[59] mentioned a more modest suggestion, that a Member's pay should continue for a month after eacn dissolution. The proposal for some sort of Member's pension is advocated in particular by those who regard present party discipline as too relentless, and the subject has been discussed in this context in Chapter IV above.

Conclusion

Life in the Palace of Westminster is still largely based on standards existing in the West End clubs of the nineteenth century. But, says a former Independent Member of Parliament, 'when it is said of the House of Commons that "it is the best club in the world", this must be taken as referring to the company, and not the comfort, of the club.'[60] Is this 'club' atmosphere desirable?

To be fair, many of the things that make life at Westminster less intolerable are due to its 'club' origin. Certainly, the principle that Members should share the House's facilities as a community, and not as a collection of factions or cliques—a principle which has had untold influence on the comparative calm of the British Parliament—stems directly from it.

The criticisms, nevertheless, remain. Many of them are caused by the physical difficulty of adapting a large and, in some ways, inefficient fabric to the needs of to-day. It is hard to say how widespread, and how deep, are these criticisms, and whether in fact they are enough to deter the best people from aiming to become Members of Parliament, or to hamper Parliament in the performance of its proper functions. It seems, on the whole, unlikely that serious complaints from a majority of the House would not be sooner or later remedied. Thus, following the various opinions expressed in the Accommodation debate of 31st March 1960, an *ad hoc* Committee was set up to advise in the matter, and the Minister of Works has given details of proposed improvements in Members' accommodation.

If the House is still affected by a nineteenth-century milieu, in one major respect at least things have changed during this century. Until the early years of this century, Members came to Westminster, having spent great sums of money in election expenses, and prepared to live as M.P.s on their private income. To-day, a Member's election expenses are rigorously controlled, and for his service in the House he receives a salary. Is this salary enough? On the one hand, a correspondent to *The Times* can say, 'Leaders in all walks of life (Burke's natural aristocrats) . . . are excluded from Parliament . . . because the present salary does not permit them to live or preserve their families from penury.'[61] On the other hand, since the House has to act as its own assessor in this matter (and perhaps feels it has to show some measure of restraint in the matter of wage advances), it clearly finds it embarrassing to grant itself an increase in pay. If the decisions in this matter were to be taken outside Parliament, at least the clumsy and perhaps rather undignified process at present used would be avoided.

Yet, important though these factors of salary and amenities may seem to be, they should not be viewed in isolation. To-day's Member of Parliament is , says *The Times*, 'overtaxed by inexorable and growing demands upon both his money and his time'.[62] It is probably this latter commodity, time, which the Member can least afford. If the character of Parliament is changing, then it is hard to disagree with the same article when it says: 'It is the pressure of business on the ordinary Member which is the fundamental cause of the change.' If this change is felt to be for the worse, then the remedy must lie in a relaxation of that pressure.

NOTES AND REFERENCES

[1] H.C. 109 of 1943–4.
[2] H.C. Deb. c. 1546, 31st March 1960.
[3] e.g. an article by A. Junz on 'Accommodation at Westminster' in *Parliamentary Affairs*, Vol. XIII, No. 1, pp. 100–13.
[4] H.C. Deb. 414, cs. 181–94; 477, 931ff.
[5] H.C. 64 of 1944/5.
[6] H.L. Deb. 172, cs. 237–54.
[7] H.C. 309 of 1952/3, and H.C. 184 of 1953/4.
[8] H.C. 184 of 1953/4, Q. 35.
[9] Readers are referred to this debate for a fuller exposition of the subject than is possible here.
[10] H.C. 64 of 1944/5, para 2.
[11] Motion, 20th July 1951.
[12] H.C. 309 of 1952/3, para 18.
[13] See below: section (*e*), part (iv).
[14] H.C. 92 of 1958/9, p. liii.
[15] *The Times*, 3rd January 1958.
[16] H.C. 184 of 1953/4.
[17] *New Statesman*, 27th February 1960, p. 278; H.C. Deb., cs. 1544–6, 31st March 1960.
[18] H.C. 276 of 1958/9.
[19] H.C. 184 of 1953/4, Evidence, Appendix D, pp. 111–13.
[20] H.C. Papers 35, 99–I of 1945/6.
[21] H.C. Deb. c. 1533, 31st March 1960. The sentiment was echoed by Gaitskell, Butler, and several other speakers in the debate.
[22] *ibid.* cs. 1537–8. See also Crick, pp. 12–13.
[23] Mrs. Castle (cs. 1538–9); Mallalieu (cs. 1579–82); Pannell (cs. 1636–7).
[24] *ibid.* cs. 1645–6.
[25] *Crossbow*, Vol. 4, No. 10, p. 14.
[26] Acland, p. 170.
[27] *How to Reform Parliament*, p. 43.
[28] H.C. 72 of 1953/4.
[29] *The Times*, 9th July 1954.
[30] *op. cit.* p. 8.
[31] *Crossbow*, Vol. 4, No. 10, p. 20.
[32] H.C. Deb. c. 1546, 31st March 1960. See also the plea for secretarial assistance by Mrs. White: *ibid.* cs. 1621–2.
[33] H.C. Deb. 310, c. 2407.
[34] H.C. 72 of 1953/4.

[35] H.C. Deb., 31st January 1958.
[36] H.C. 92 of 1958/9, p. liii; Q. 564.
[37] H.C. Deb. 617, c. 132.
[38] H.C. Deb. c. 1536, 31st March 1960.
[39] H.C. 64 of 1944/5.
[40] e.g. H.C. Deb. 477, c. 26 (Sir H. Williams).
[41] H.C. 309 of 1952/3, Report, paras. 18–19.
[42] H.C. Deb. cs. 1632–3, 31st March 1960.
[43] H.C. Deb. cs. 678–9, 23rd June 1960.
[44] A Member's annual salary has been, since 4th April 1957, £1,750. Of this sum, the average sum allowable as 'necessary expenses' by the Income Tax authorities seems to be about £750.
[45] H.C. 92 of 1958/9, Q. 518–19.
[46] *Crossbow*, Vol. 4, No. 10, p. 11.
[47] H.C. 72 of 1953/4.
[48] H.C. Deb., 528, cs. 30–158.
[49] The expenses generally spoken of in this context are those for secretarial help, correspondence and the running of a car. (H.C. 72 of 1953/4.)
[50] *The Times*, 9th July 1954.
[51] Crick, pp. 7–8.
[52] e.g. *The Times*, 22nd February 1954. (Letter from H. Wiseman.)
[53] *The Times*, 1st March 1954. (Letter from J. Foley.)
[54] *The Times*, 28th May 1954. (Letter from Sir A. Herbert.)
[55] *The Times*, 8th March 1954.
[56] *The Times*, 28th May 1954.
[57] Acland, p. 170.
[58] *Parliamentary Representation*, p. 209.
[59] H.C. 72 of 1953/4.
[60] The late W. J. Brown: *Everybody's Guide to Parliament*, 1945, p. 80.
[61] H. Maddick, *The Times*, 24th February 1954; the annual salary was then £1,000.
[62] *The Times*, 8th March 1954.

APPENDIX

The Reform of the House of Lords

INTRODUCTION

This short appendix is written to deal only with proposals for the *reform* of the House of Lords; the arguments of some political thinkers in our period in favour of *abolishing* the second House seem now to be rather hollow. The moment of truth for the House of Lords came in 1945, when a radical Government came into power with a large majority and with no love for the *status quo*. The fact that the House survived, with its composition unchanged (though with its powers constricted) shows that—at least for the time being—the abolitionists' cause is not a practical proposition.

Another theoretical matter on which sides were still being taken in the thirties was whether the second House should be 'strong'— that is, as strong as the Commons—or only 'useful'; but controversy on this point, too, seems a little lame to-day. Campion has pointed out that, now that the Second Chamber has become another field for the evolution of political parties, the 'strong' Chamber has little value. If its political colour is the same as the other House, its concurrence in that House's view can be taken for granted; if its colour is different, it will block the other House's proposals. Thus a 'strong' Second Chamber is, in the one event, superfluous and, in the other, mischievous. The same does not apply to a 'useful' Second Chamber which, since it cannot seriously challenge the other House, can perform its minor but valuable functions in a spirit of objectivity.[1]

In practice as in theory, the House of Lords falls in the category of 'useful' Second Chambers. Its powers in regard to finance have for centuries been inferior to those of the Commons, and the Parliament Act, 1911, reduced its equality in the field of legislation to a two-year delaying power. In 1949, this limit of delay was reduced to one year.

For Notes and References see page 180

APPENDIX

(*a*) THE HOUSE'S POWERS

Peter Bromhead avers that some Conservatives still believe in a House of Lords with greater powers. They believe it possible for a Government to lose the support of the majority of the electorate long before a General Election, so that bills passed by the Commons towards the end of a Parliament may not accord at all with the popular will; thus there is a case for allowing the Lords a greater stopping-power.[2] An article in *Crossbow* has recently said that it would be no bad thing if the Commons met a little more competition from the House of Lords. It suggests that that House could usefully be duplicated, with a House of Scottish peers in Edinburgh.[3]

On the other hand, official Conservative opinion seems to have acquiesced in the present curtailment of the Lords' powers. Lord Salisbury spoke (somewhat guardedly) for his Party in March 1955, saying that although they would not wish 'to tie themselves to the proposition that in no circumstances should any House of Lords, however constituted, have any more powers than . . . today, . . . [yet] it is more immediately necessary to deal with the reform of the composition than with . . . the powers of the House'.[4]

From the left-wing come occasional suggestions for reducing the powers of the Lords still further; thus Anthony Wedgwood Benn has spoken of a delaying power of three months for the Lords,[5] and has proposed that they should have no say in the affirming or negating of Statutory Instruments.[6] Subsequently, his own elevation to the peerage has reopened the whole subject of House of Lords reform.

(*b*) THE HOUSE'S COMPOSITION

It will be noted that Lord Salisbury (in the quotation above), while not advising any change in the powers of the Lords, thought that reform of the composition of that House was more immediately necessary. It is this aspect of the problem which raises most interest nowadays.[7]

One of the major criticisms of the present House is that the so-called 'backwoodsmen' can come down and flood the House with their votes at any time. Thus it was proposed by Lord Exeter that peers who failed to attend debates with reasonable regularity should be excluded from the right to vote.[8] Although this motion was not accepted, it has been followed by the passing of a new Standing Order[9] under which peers are asked whether or not they wish to apply for leave of absence from the House.[10] Those who do, or those who fail to answer within a month, are not expected to attend until their leave of absence has been terminated. Lord Simon's bill in 1953 was adjourned in the hope that discussions between the party leaders might result in agreement on the whole subject of reform of the Lords.[11] This hope proved abortive, and when the Government introduced its Life Peerages Bill in 1957, it was opposed (in the Commons) by the Labour Opposition. On passing into law, however, the Opposition agreed to nominate some of the first life peers; and within three years of its enactment, a commentator has said that the act has been so successful that it ought to be much more extensively used.[12]

The principle that the heir to a peerage might, by the accident of death, have to give up a career in the House of Commons, has been attacked on several occasions—most recently by two people personally affected, Lord Hailsham and Wedgwood Benn. Lord Ponsonby, in 1936, unsuccessfully moved that peers should be allowed to vote at General Elections and be themselves eligible for election to the Commons (in which case they would forfeit their right to sit in the Lords).[13] Wedgwood Benn introduced, in 1955, a bill to renounce his right to a peerage, without affecting the right of his children, in their turn, to succeed. This bill was rejected on Second Reading in the Lords.[14] The major argument against these proposals is always that it would deprive the House of Lords of some of its ablest material.

The arguments to admit women to the House of Lords are obvious and well-known; attempts to do so have been made for a long while.[15] They have been of two general kinds; either attempts to allow peeresses in their own right to take their seats, or attempts to confer life peerages on women, and so enable them to sit in the Lords. The former attempts have never got over the decision of the Committee of Privileges (in the case of Lady Rhondda) in 1922 that women had no right to sit in the Lords, and the hostility of the Labour Party as a whole to any extension of the hereditary element in the Lords. The latter attempts, however, have been finally successful, and the first group of peerages under the Life Peerages Act, 1958, included three women.

A small piece of reform—not directly concerned with the composition of the Lords, though it may influence peers in their decision whether or not to ask for leave of absence from the House—is the payment of peers. Since 1946, peers regularly attending the House have been reimbursed for their travelling expenses. Since 1957, an expense allowance of three guineas per day has been claimable by peers; this, however, has been attacked by some peers as being quite inadequate.[16]

There have been a number of proposals put forward for a wholesale change in the composition of the House of Lords. Bromhead lists five main ideas, and says that most of the compendious proposals for reform of representation in the Lords combine two or more of these five. They are:

(i) Some members should be elected on a regional basis (as are at present Scottish representative peers). Electoral colleges might be composed of members of local authorities.

(ii) Some Members should be elected by the House of Commons by some sort of proportional representation, and probably for long periods.

(iii) Some Members should be elected by and from the holders of existing peerages.

(iv) Some Members should be appointed by the Crown, on nomination by the Government, or by the Government and the Opposition.

(v) Some Members should be appointed to represent specific associations and other bodies.[17]

A bill introduced by Salisbury in 1933 aimed to implement the majority proposals of the Bryce Conference (which had sat some fifteen years earlier). This had envisaged 246 members elected by Members of the House of Commons, and eighty elected by a joint committee of both Houses; the latter element would always contain a total of at least thirty hereditary peers and bishops. The election would be for twelve years, with one-third retiring every four years. This bill was duly read a second time, but made no further progress. The Bryce Conference recommendations were also favoured by the authors of a Fabian Society pamphlet, who, however, thought that the total number should be little more than one hundred.[18]

During the passage of the Parliament Act, 1949, an all-party conference attempted to reach agreement on the possibility of reform. Although this subsequently broke down over the question of the extent of the delaying power of the Lords, it agreed on certain basic principles. One of these was that the House's composition should never assure a permanent majority to one political party (as is at present the case). During the debates, Lord Cecil of Chelwood put forward a scheme that the composition of the House should remain unchanged, but that on legislative matters only 200 members should be allowed to vote; these 200 would be chosen in such a way as to give the parties fair representation.

A new scheme for the reform of the Lords was put forward in 1957 by Wedgwood Benn.[19] This proposed that the Second Chamber should be composed of all members of the Privy Council who do not sit in the Commons. At the beginning of 1957, this would have given a House of 206 members (125 peers and eighty-one others). Bromhead points out that, although this scheme has advantages, it means that the Lords would consist only of distinguished men, many of whom may be elderly; there would be none of the fairly young, able men who at present do much of the work of the House.[20]

Lord Salisbury, in a letter to *The Times*, has suggested that a reformed House should consist of life peers together with some 200 hereditary peers chosen by a Select Committee at the beginning of each Parliament.[21]

Conclusion

There seems widespread agreement to-day that we need a second chamber of some kind, and that it should be 'useful'—that is to say, subordinate and objective—rather than 'strong'. All proposals for reform of the House of Lords fall into two categories—those which aspire to change its powers, and those directed against its composition. It may be that successive Governments, while they have been vocal enough on the subject when

in Opposition, have been hesitant to tackle the problem firmly
in case they should seem to be guilty of gerrymandering. Whatever
the reason, the 1945–50 Government did not bring forward any
scheme for the re-composition of the House (which, as the 1948
all-party conference showed, everyone agreed was necessary).
They did, however, restrict the powers of the House in such a
way as, it now seems, to be agreeable to the main parties.

So it is to the personnel of the House that most schemes of
Lords' reform now direct themselves. The House, with its 870 or
so peers, is, said Lord Samuel, 'the only institution in the world
which is kept going by the persistent absenteeism of the great
majority of its members'.[22] A major weakness in its functionings is
admittedly the way those persistent absentees may, on a particular
legislative proposal, swamp the Lords with their votes, and thereby
thwart the will of the Commons. Yet a major source of strength
is the fact that it contains, amongst those habitual absentees,
experts who will come and advise the House with their wisdom on
the rare occasions when their own subject is in dispute. The
dilemma of the House of Lords is that it needs its large composition when it is acting as a deliberative body, but that it cannot
afford them when it acts legislatively.

In these circumstances, there is clearly something to be said for
the principle of restricting the right of voting, on legislative matters
only, to a certain number; Bromhead favours this.[23] But this
proposal, by itself, does not do away with the basic archaism by
which important decisions are taken by people whose only claim
to distinction is that they are descended from a forebear who did
some service to the State. On this ground, the supporters of Life
Peerages may feel that their proposal offers what is needed.

The Life Peerages Act, 1958, met with no great enthusiasm;
it was felt to make no serious attempt to get to the heart of the
matter. Yet it established a new principle, and its effects may have
been underestimated. Certainly—with life peerages, the payment
of peers, the admission of women into the House, and the voluntary
exclusion of some non-attenders—there have been some considerable changes in the House of Lords in the last few years. The
'tired waves' may still seem to be 'vainly breaking', but it could
be that the tide is on the turn.

179

APPENDIX

NOTES AND REFERENCES

[1] *Parliamentary Affairs*, Vol. VII, No. 1.
[2] Bromhead, *The House of Lords and Contemporary Politics*, 1958, pp. 242–3.
[3] *Crossbow*, Vol. 4 No. 10, p. 8.
[4] H.L. Deb. 191, c. 855.
[5] *The Privy Council as a Second Chamber*, Fabian Tract, No. 305.
[6] H.C. Bill 60 of 1957/8 (Bill to alter the composition of the House of Lords).
[7] Much of what follows is taken from Bromhead, *op. cit.*
[8] H.L. Deb., 181, cs. 5–9, 17th March 1953.
[9] S.O. 21.
[10] When the new Standing Order came into force, about one in five peers applied for leave of absence for the rest of the Parliament.
[11] H.L. Deb. 180, cs. 251–4.
[12] *Crossbow*, Vol. 4, No. 10, p. 8.
[13] H.L. Deb. 99, cs. 536 ff.
[14] H.L. Deb. 192, cs. 563–94.
[15] e.g., Iwi, *Parliamentary Affairs*, Vol. VII, No. 1.
[16] See the debates on the Life Peerages Bill in the Lords in 1957, *passim*.
[17] Bromhead, pp. 259–60. The author points out that little has been heard of this last idea in recent years.
[18] *Reform of the Lords*, Fabian Research Series, No. 169, 1954.
[19] *The Privy Council as a Second Chamber*, Fabian Tract, No. 305.
[20] Bromhead, pp. 269–70.
[21] On 12th November 1957.
[22] H.L. Deb., 153, c. 656.
[23] Bromhead, p. 269.

Selected Bibliography

Books and pamphlets only are listed below. References to *Hansard*, Parliamentary Papers and other *official* publications, and to articles, newspaper reports, etc., are given in the notes to the text. The books listed below do *not* constitute a bibliography on Parliament: they are essentially the main sources (other than official publications) from which the preceding study on *Parliamentary Reform* has been compiled. A good recent bibliography on Parliament has been compiled for the Hansard Society by J. H. Palmer: *Government and Parliament in Britain* (1960).

Where a book included in the list below is referred to frequently in the text, the footnote reference is normally given in shortened form, thus: Acland, p. 137. Shortened forms of this type are avoided in cases where more than one book by a particular author is listed below.

Acland, Sir R., *What It Will be Like in the New Britain*. Gollancz Ltd., 1942.

Acton Society Trust. *Nationalised Industry*. (*1*) *Accountability to Parliament*. (*2*) *Powers of the Minister*. Acton Society Trust, 1950.

Allen, Sir C. K., *Law and Orders*, 2nd ed. Stevens & Sons Ltd., 1956.

Amery, L. S., *Thoughts on the Constitution*. O.U.P., 1947.

Attlee, C. R. (Lord Attlee), *As It Happened*. Heinemann Ltd., 1954.

Bailey, S. D. (ed.), *The British Party System: A Symposium*. Hansard Society, 1952.

Bailey, S. D. (ed.), *The Future of the House of Lords: A Symposium*. Hansard Society, 1954.

Barker, Sir E., *Reflections on Government*. O.U.P., 1953 (1942).

Benn, A. Wedgwood, *The Privy Council as a Second Chamber*. Fabian Tract, 305, 1957.

Black, D., *The Theory of Committees and Elections*. C.U.P., 1958.

Bromhead, P. A., *The House of Lords and Contemporary Politics*, *1911–1957*. Routledge & Kegan Paul Ltd., 1958.

Bromhead, P. A., *Private Members' Bills in the British Parliament*. Routledge & Kegan Paul Ltd., 1956.

Bulmer-Thomas, I., *The Party System in Great Britain*. Phoenix House Ltd., 1953.

Butler, D. E., *The Electoral System in Britain 1918–1951*. O.U.P., 1953.

Butler, D. E. and others. *Elections Abroad*. Macmillan & Co. Ltd., 1959.

Butler, D. E. & Rose, R., *The British General Election of 1959*. Macmillan & Co. Ltd., 1960.

Campion, Lord. *An Introduction to the Procedure of the House of Commons*, 3rd ed. Macmillan & Co. Ltd., 1958.

Campion, Lord, and others. *Parliament: A Survey*. G. Allen & Unwin Ltd., 1952.

Carter, B. E., *The Office of Prime Minister*. Faber & Faber Ltd., 1956.

Chorley, Lord, and others. *Reform of the Lords*. Fabian Research Series, 169, 1954.

Chubb, B., *The Control of Public Expenditure*. O.U.P., 1952.

Constitutional Reform. *Some Proposals for Constitutional Reform: being the Recommendations of a Group of Conservatives*. Eyre & Spottiswoode Ltd., 1946.

Crick, B., *Reform of the Commons*. Fabian Tract, 319, 1959.

Curtis, M. R., *Central Government: An Introduction*. Pitman & Sons Ltd., 1956.

Duverger, M., *Political Parties: Their Organisation and Activity in the Modern State*. (Translated by B. & R. North), 2nd ed. rev., Methuen & Co. Ltd., 1959.

Einzig, P., *The Control of the Purse: progress and decline of Parliament's Financial Control*. Secker & Warburg Ltd., 1959.

Finer, H., *The Theory and Practice of Modern Government*. Methuen & Co. Ltd., 1954.

Finer, S. E., *Anonymous Empire: A Study of the 'Lobby' in Great Britain*. Pall Mall Press, 1958.

Foot, M., *Parliament in Danger!* Pall Mall Press, 1959.

Gaitskell, H., *In Defence of Politics*. Birkbeck College, 1954.

Gordon, S., *Our Parliament*, 5th ed. Hansard Society, 1958.

Granada TV. *A First Report on Constituency Television in a General Election.* Granada TV Network, 1959.

Greaves, H. R. G., *The British Constitution.* 2nd ed., G. Allen & Unwin Ltd., 1948.

Harrison, W., *The Government of Britain.* Hutchinson & Co. Ltd., 1948.

Herbert, Sir A. P., *Independent Member.* Methuen & Co. Ltd., 1950.

Herbert, Sir A. P., *I Object: Letter to the Electors of East Harrow.* Bodley Head Ltd., 1958.

Hollis, C., *Can Parliament Survive?* Hollis & Carter, 1949.

Hollis, C., *Has Parliament a Future?* Unservile State Papers No. 1, 1960.

Howarth, P., *Questions in the House.* Bodley Head Ltd., 1956.

Institute of Electoral Research. *A review of Elections 1954–1958.* Inst. of Electoral Research, 1960.

Iwi, E. F., *Laws and Flaws: Lapses of the Legislators.* Odhams Press Ltd., 1956.

Jennings, Sir W. I., *Cabinet Government,* 3rd ed., C.U.P., 1959.

Jennings, Sir W. I., *Parliament,* 2nd ed., C.U.P., 1957.

Jennings, Sir W. I., *Parliament Must be Reformed: A Programme for Democratic Government.* Kegan Paul, Trench, Trubner & Co. Ltd., 1941.

Jennings, Sir W. I., *Parliamentary Reform.* Gollancz Ltd. (for the New Fabian Research Bureau), 1934.

Jennings, Sir W. I., *Party Politics I: Appeal to the People.* C.U.P., 1960; II: *Growth of Parties.* C.U.P., 1961.

Keeton, G. W., *The Passing of Parliament,* 2nd ed., Ernest Benn Ltd., 1954.

Kelf-Cohen, R., *Nationalisation in Britain: The End of a Dogma.* Macmillan & Co. Ltd., 1958.

Lakeman, E. & Lambert, J. D., *Voting in Democracies.* Faber & Faber Ltd., 1955.

Laski, H. J., *Reflections on the Constitution.* M.U.P., 1951.

Le May, G. H. L., *British Government 1914–1953: Select Documents.* Methuen & Co. Ltd., 1955.

Mackay, R. W. G., *Coupon or Free? Being a Study in Electoral Reform and Representative Government.* Secker & Warburg Ltd., 1943.

McKenzie, R. T., *British Political Parties*, Heinemann Ltd., 1955.

Marshall, G. & Moodie, G. C., *Some Problems of the Constitution*. Hutchinson & Co. Ltd., 1959.

Mathiot, A., *The British Political System*. Trans. by J. S. Hines. Hogarth Press Ltd., 1958.

Morrison, H. S. (Lord Morrison of Lambeth). *Government and Parliament: A Survey from the Inside*. O.U.P., 1954. (2nd. ed., 1959).

Muir, R., *How Britain is Governed: A Critical Analysis of Modern Developments in the British System of Government*, 2nd ed. Constable & Co. Ltd., 1930.

Nicolson, N., *People and Parliament*. Weidenfeld & Nicolson Ltd., 1958.

Pollard, R. S. W., *How to Reform Parliament*. Forum Press, 1944. *Speed-Up Law Reform*. Fabian Research Series, 194, 1958.

Richards, P. G., *Honourable Members: A Study of the British Backbencher*. Faber & Faber Ltd., 1959.

Ross, J. F. S., *The Achievement of Representative Democracy*. Bowes & Bowes Ltd., 1952.

Ross, J. F. S., *Elections and Electors: Studies in Democratic Representation*. Eyre & Spottiswoode Ltd., 1955.

Ross, J. F. S., *Parliamentary Representation*. 2nd. ed., Eyre & Spottiswoode Ltd., 1948.

Shinwell, E., *The Britain I Want*. (Chapt. XV: Parliament and Democracy), Macdonald & Co. Ltd., 1943.

Spearman, D., *Democracy in England*. Barrie & Rockliff, 1957.

Stewart, J. D., *British Pressure Groups: Their Role in Relation to the House of Commons*. O.U.P., 1958.

Stewart, M., *The British Approach to Politics*, 3rd ed. rev. G. Allen & Unwin Ltd., 1955.

Thomas, H. (ed.), *The Establishment: A Symposium*. Anthony Blond Ltd., 1959.

Watson, G. (ed.), *The Unservile State: Essays in Liberty and Welfare*. G. Allen & Unwin Ltd., 1957.

Index

N*